Excellence & Equity

EXCELLENCE & EQUITY

The National Endowment
for the Humanities

STEPHEN MILLER

THE UNIVERSITY PRESS OF KENTUCKY

Copyright © 1984 by The University Press of Kentucky

Scholarly publisher for the Commonwealth, serving Bellarmine College, Berea College, Centre College of Kentucky, Eastern Kentucky University, The Filson Club, Georgetown College, Kentucky Historical Society, Kentucky State University, Morehead State University, Murray State University, Northern Kentucky University, Transylvania University, University of Kentucky, University of Louisville, and Western Kentucky University.

Editorial Offices: Lexington, Kentucky 40506-0024

Library of Congress Cataloging in Publication Data

Miller, Stephen, 1941–
    Excellence and equity.

    Includes bibliographical references and index.
    1. National Endowment for the Humanities—Evaluation.
I. Title.
HV97.N336M54   1984   353.9'3854   83-21861
ISBN 0-8131-1504-3

To Eva, Katherine, and Elizabeth

CONTENTS

ACKNOWLEDGMENTS

I SHOULD LIKE to thank Marc Plattner, who suggested that I undertake this study, and the Twentieth Century Fund, which provided support for this project. A number of people made my work easier. Robert Kingston, Jeffrey Field, and Leonard Oliver were especially helpful in providing information about NEH. Sir Isaiah Berlin, Edward Shils, and Robert S. Lapiner provided me with useful information about the support of the humanities in Western Europe. In response to my numerous requests for information, the staff of NEH was unfailingly courteous.

The manuscript benefited from the suggestions of Theodore Draper, James Banner, John William Ward, James Smith, and Marcia Bystryn. Finally, I am very grateful for the editorial suggestions of Margaret Gwynne, which were invaluable.

INTRODUCTION

IN MAY 1981 President Reagan announced the formation of a blue-ribbon task force whose main purpose would be to find ways to increase private support for the arts and the humanities. The Reagan administration maintained that increased private contributions would compensate for the dramatic reduction—approximately 50 percent—in the budgets of the National Endowment for the Humanities (NEH) and the National Endowment for the Arts (NEA) that it had recommended to Congress in February 1981.

There was little support for the cuts in Congress, and the two agencies received appropriations only slightly lower than those of the previous year. But many of those concerned with the arts and the humanities were troubled by the apparent vulnerability of NEH and NEA, fearing that the sizes of the proposed cuts, larger than those recommended for most federal agencies, suggested that the arts and the humanities were being singled out for attack. Some even suspected that the formation of Reagan's task force meant that the agencies' very right to exist was being questioned. At the annual meeting of the American Council of Learned Societies, an organization that had played a major role in the formation of NEH, John E. Sawyer, president of the Andrew J. Mellon Foundation, remarked that "in light of progress made and lessons learned since the founding of the National Endowments for the Arts and Humanities in 1965, it is troubling that a special task force was required to persuade those now in power of the enduring value of substantial federal support of these fields."[1]

Criticism of NEH and NEA was by no means confined to the Reagan administration. The agencies were also taken to task by certain journalists who doubted that support of the arts and the humanities was a legitimate function of government. Robert Samuelson, a columnist for the *National Journal*, asked: "Do we really need the government to subsidize high-brow entertainment—theater, ballet, opera and television drama—and to promote vacuous ideals such as better public understanding of the humanities?"[2] In the same vein, Lewis Lapham, the former editor of *Harper's*, argued that "the huge sums distributed through the National Endowments and the Corporation for Public Broadcasting . . . constitute a donative to the upper middle class. . . . The exegesis of the so-called high culture provides sinecures for the younger sons of the capitalist nobility, for the *nouveaux littéraires*, and for the ladies or gentlemen too refined for commerce and trade."[3] And Donald Lambro—in *Fat City*, a book that surveys the landscape of federal programs and argues that many of them are a waste of the taxpayer's money—termed both NEH and NEA "non-essential."[4]

Most of the theoretical arguments about the propriety of federal support centered on the arts rather than the humanities. In *The Public Interest*, for example, Tom Bethell argued that "arts-funding is in practice an income-transfer program for the upper-middle-class."[5] And in *Policy Review*, Ernest Van Den Haag declared the arts undeserving of federal support because they "are not among the activities which contribute enough to social cohesion, national identity, or shared values in the U.S."[6] Since NEH and NEA are often perceived as being closely linked, such attacks usually imply condemnation of the humanities endowment as well. For the most part, however, critics who have considered NEH specifically have not questioned the agency's right to exist; rather, they have attacked the policies it has pursued.

In the late 1970s, the most influential and insistent critic of NEH was probably Hilton Kramer, who was the cultural editor of the *New York Times* when Joseph Duffey was chairman of NEH. Although Kramer believed that federal support for the humanities was appropriate, in 1977 he expressed dismay over the appointment of Duffey, fearing that under Duffey's chairmanship the agency would be, as Kramer put it, politicized. By 1980 Kramer believed his apprehensions had proven well founded, for he argued that "the activities of both Endowments have been profoundly compromised by politicization and an accompanying lowering of standards."[7] A 1980 report by a distinguished commission on the humanities, chaired by Richard W. Lyman, the president of the Rockefeller Foundation, agreed with Kramer to some extent. Though the report, *The Humanities in American Life* (hereafter referred to as the *1980 Report*), generally praised the work of NEH, it also said that NEH has "sometimes politicized the humanities, to the dismay of humanists, politicians, and Endowment officials."[8] Not surprisingly, members of Reagan's transition team and Republican contenders for Duffey's position voiced similar sentiments. And while Duffey of course disagreed with them, even he expressed reservations about the agency's work. In 1981 he admitted that "both Endowments have grown too quickly. . . . Areas nobody questions are riding high."[9]

In this study of NEH, I am in agreement with the most basic assumption of both Kramer and Duffey—that NEH should continue to exist. This assumption, however, begs a multitude of questions about the agency's goals and procedures as well as about the appropriate level of federal support. This book will focus closely on both the "areas nobody questions" and the issues that have prompted serious disagreements among those who are concerned about the future of NEH.

One question deserving of consideration is whether NEH has grown too quickly and has, as a result, thrown money at dubious programs and projects; that is, whether it has turned into a new kind of pork barrel. In *Nostromo*, Joseph Conrad asks if "there is something inherent in the necessities of successful action which carries with it the moral degradation of the idea."[10] Have the "necessities of successful action" on the part of NEH—the need to win friends in Congress and to build a constituency for its programs—made it difficult for the agency to adhere to its mandate to support "national progress and scholarship in the humanities"?

A second issue in need of examination is the increasing extent to which discussion about the purposes of NEH has become politically partisan. The agency was founded in 1965 with bipartisan support, yet since 1976 it has often been discussed in partisan terms, almost as if there were distinct Democratic and Republican approaches to federal support for the humanities. Should the agency, as many Democratic observers urge, actively seek out grantees and award funds to those who might profit in some way from exposure to the humanities? Or should it, as many Republican observers argue, refrain altogether from soliciting applications and instead concentrate on supporting those projects whose merit is most convincingly demonstrated by applicants? These different emphases bear upon the larger questions of equality and affirmative action, often the subjects of heated political debate.

But to dwell exclusively on the politicization of NEH would be to obscure an equally difficult problem under which the agency has labored since its inception: clarifying its mandate. No doubt many federal agencies have come into being with only vague authorizing legislation, so that their mandates are unclear, but NEH suffers additionally from having been born a twin to NEA. As a result, it is usually assumed, both in Congress and in the press, that NEH and NEA should be discussed together. But some observers, including several who played major roles in the founding of NEH, believe that the comparison with NEA is misleading and that the true counterpart of NEH is the National Science Foundation (NSF). The distinction is important because NSF is oriented toward research. If NEH were perceived to be the same kind of agency as NSF, its primary mission would obviously be to support research rather than to gain a large audience for the humanities, as NEA has attempted to do for the arts. Few observers would suggest that NEH should devote itself exclusively either to public programs or to research, but there is much disagreement about which concern should have priority, and this issue has spawned further disagreement about the way NEH should allocate its funds. It has also resulted in disagreements about the roles the chairman and staff should play in the agency. If NEH is to gain an audience for the humanities, then the chairman and the staff must take a more active part in the grant-making process, seeking out organizations capable of mounting public programs and assisting them with their applications.

Such fundamental disagreements about its mandate have bedeviled NEH, for it often finds itself in a crossfire of criticism, attacked both by those who think it has gone too far in a given direction and by those who think it has not gone far enough. Yet it is evident that its confusing mandate has not been an impossible burden, for in many ways NEH has proven to be a modest success. In this book both the strengths and the weaknesses of the agency are assessed.

The focus is on two broad questions: how NEH's identity problem has affected its development, and how effective its programs have been in promoting scholarship and humanistic education and in increasing public appreciation of the humanities. The book includes both an attempt to gauge the potential contribution of the private sector in support of the humanities and an examination of a number of ideas that, if adopted, may make NEH more effective as a force for progress and scholarship in the humanities.

1

The Founding of NEH

AT CONGRESSIONAL hearings held during the winter of 1965, Senator Ernest Gruening of Alaska, a man whom his colleague Claiborne Pell called "the spearhead of this humanities bill," reminded Congress that "there is nothing as inevitable as an idea whose time has arrived."[1] He was quoting Victor Hugo to describe the remarkable showing of congressional support for legislation to provide federal aid for the arts and the humanities—legislation that moved through the 89th Congress with relative ease. On March 10, 1965, the Johnson administration's bill to create a National Foundation for the Arts and the Humanities was simultaneously introduced into the Senate and the House by Senator Pell and Representative Frank Thompson of New Jersey. On September 29 of that year the bill, only slightly modified, was signed into law. Federal support for the arts and the humanities was indeed an idea whose time had arrived.

It had arrived quite suddenly. For fifteen years or so there had been some support in Congress and the executive branch for aid to the arts, but nothing had been said about the humanities until 1964. In the summer of that year a national commission on the humanities, supported by the American Council of Learned Societies (ACLS), the Council of Graduate Schools in the United States, and the United Chapters of Phi Beta Kappa, issued a report calling for the creation of a national humanities foundation. The *Report of the Commission on the Humanities* (hereinafter called the *1964 Report*), greeted with enthusiasm by the *New York Times* and *Science* magazine, led almost immediately to the introduction of a bill in the House to establish a national humanities foundation. An editorial in *Science* predicted that it would be no easy task to persuade Congress to establish such a foundation. "It took five years of effort to bring the National Science Foundation into being," the editorial warned, "and it does not appear that a National Humanities Foundation will be any easier to establish."[2] Only six months later, however, in January 1965, *Science* declared that "prospects look bright" for such a foundation, since "no public word of opposition has been raised to the principle of the federal government's assuming some financial responsibility for the arts and the humanities."[3] Shortly thereafter a bill to establish a humanities foundation, introduced by Representative William S. Moorhead of Pennsylvania, gained eighty-seven cosponsors (seventy-two Democrats and fifteen Republicans)—more, it was claimed, than any other legislative proposal then before the House.[4]

Without the *1964 Report*, it is doubtful that a National Endowment for the Humanities would have been created. When Senator Pell introduced the administration's bill, he praised the *1964 Report* for "helping form the basis for the legislation I have already presented,"[5] referring to a bill similar to the administration's that he had introduced earlier in the session. Yet surely it was not the *1964 Report* alone that spurred so many congressmen to support the creation of NEH; innumerable reports by innumerable commissions have proposed legislative actions subsequently ignored by Congress. And rarely, if ever, had a recommendation been acted upon so quickly that the idea became reality in less than a year and a half.

The *1964 Report* was successful in part because it reflected the belief of many journalists, academics, and congressmen that a Great Society (to use President Johnson's phrase) should recognize, honor, and foster excellence in the humanities as well as the sciences. As historian John Higham, summing up the temper of the times (or the temper, at least, of the nation's professional classes), pointed out: "Each year the National Science Foundation, which [was] . . . created in 1950, pours greater sums into the hands of scientists engaged in 'basic research'. . . . Surely, in the midst of so much affluence, such hunger for excellence, so much concern about the quality of American culture, the humanities need not remain unassisted."[6] Senator Pell agreed. On June 10, when the administration's bill was reported out of committee, Pell declared that the new legislation would "help greatly to give the arts and humanities their rightful place of honor in our society."[7]

In speaking about the humanities' "rightful place of honor," Senator Pell was not implying that the sciences were honored too much but rather that the humanities were not honored enough. During the early 1960s the sciences by and large were held in high esteem; it was not until the late 1960s, as a result of the war in Vietnam, that scientists came under increasing attack as the alleged handmaidens of the military. In the early 1960s there was less concern about the inhumane products of scientific research than about the possibility of an intellectual climate in which scientists alone were honored and scientific education alone given governmental support. "The nation's need for balanced education demands that this imbalance be remedied," the *1964 Report* argued.[8] At the congressional hearings, Frederick Burkhardt, then president of the ACLS, maintained that "a lopsided, half-starved educational system is something this country simply cannot afford. . . . Science itself will suffer in such a culture."[9] During the course of congressional debate on the administration's bill, numerous congressmen invoked this notion of imbalance. It reflected a situation, they warned, that might prove dangerous to the health of the nation.

At times the remarks of those who called for federal support for the humanities were tinged with resentment that scholars in the humanities were being ignored by the government. Speculating about what had led to the formation of the Commission on the Humanities, Fred Hechinger, education editor of the *New York Times*, noted in 1964 that "there has been much grumbling in the non-scientific camp of American education."[10] Hechinger pointed out that the gap between the scientific haves and the humanistic have-nots had been widening continually. An observer in the *New York Times Magazine* concurred, claiming that students and professors of the humanities "find themselves inhabiting a dingy academic slum with modest research grants, or none, lower salaries, and few of the gaudy emoluments—travel and consulting—which have recently glamorized other branches of academic life."[11] Few scholars in the humanities in the early 1960s felt that the federal government should withdraw its support of scientists; rather, most agreed with Barnaby Keeney, the president of Brown University, who had served as chairman of the Commission on the Humanities, that "the scientists have their Foundation; the humanists should have theirs."[12]

But it was not until 1963, a full thirteen years after NSF had been established, that the Commission on the Humanities was formed with the express purpose of recommending a national humanities foundation. Why had it taken so long for scholars in the humanities to organize in this fashion? Several reasons come to mind. Scholars in the humanities, unlike many scientists, had only rarely done research for the federal government during World War II and were not inclined to look upon government as their natural ally. Scholars in the humanities, unlike scientists, rarely collaborated on projects, and it was perhaps difficult or even distasteful for them to band together to lobby for government funds. Finally, scholars in the humanities were less dependent than scientists on large infusions of money with which to carry on their research.

There may have been two other, somewhat less obvious, reasons as well. Some scholars, probably many, were both puzzled and made uncomfortable by the term "humanities." Reviewing a book entitled *The Humanities at Work*, Lionel Trilling had observed in 1944 that "nobody quite knows what they [the humanities] are." Two decades later Northrop Frye suggested that "after more than a century of giving answers to the question of what is distinctive about the humanities, it is still quite possible that the real answer is 'nothing at all.'"[13] To this day few scholars in the humanities call themselves humanists, preferring to think of themselves as members of particular disciplines—historians, literary critics, philosophers, and so on. Second, some scholars in the humanities (how many it is impossible to say) looked down with genteel disdain upon the world of politics; they would not demean themselves by banding together to seek recognition from the federal government. If Washington did not recognize and appreciate what they were doing, this was to them a reflection only of the philistinism of American culture.

In any case, the 1950s were not an opportune time to call for government support of the humanities. The cold war and the 1957 launching of Sputnik caused Congress and the nation in general to become preoccupied with the quality of American science. "How much money would you need to . . . make us even with Russia?"[14] Representative James C. Fulton of Pennsylvania asked the chairman of the National Aeronautics and Space Administration (NASA), which was established in 1958. Between 1957 and 1960, federal expenditures for research and development in science more than doubled, and there was an even greater increase in outlays for basic research to not-for-profit institutions. Some of the increased appropriations did go to the humanities: in 1958 Congress passed the National Defense Education Act, providing support for students in the humanities as well as the sciences, but the major concern, as the title of the act implies, was America's military capability. What the nation needed to improve that capability, President Eisenhower declared in 1958, was more scientists—"thousands more" in the next ten years than the nation was currently planning to produce.[15] The fear that the Soviet Union was moving ahead of the United States in scientific and military know-how prompted a tremendous increase in the budget for NSF: the last pre-Sputnik appropriation was $40 million; the first post-Sputnik appropriation, $130 million.

By the mid-1960s, however, congressional enthusiasm for science had waned considerably, so much so that in January 1966 Philip Abelson, the editor of *Science*, lamented that "a twenty-year honeymoon for science is drawing to a close."[16] The new disenchantment was the inevitable result of the enthusiastic commitment to science in the 1950s. According to historian Daniel Kevles, "the sheer bigness of Big Science was enough to arouse questions" about whether the sciences were having too great an impact on American life.[17] Was the nation, President Eisenhower asked in his farewell address, in danger of becoming "the captive of a scientific-technological elite?"[18]

At the same time, many scholars in the humanities were coming to think of themselves as part of a distinctive "culture," a notion promoted by C.P. Snow in *The Two Cultures and the Scientific Revolution* (1959). Snow's contention that the work of the humanistic culture had become largely irrelevant to the problems of contemporary life drew a good deal of fire from scholars in the humanities. If the most vituperative outburst was that of F.R. Leavis, the English literary critic who heaped scorn on Snow's literary achievement and intellectual outlook, the most sharply drawn was that of Lionel Trilling, who (noting Snow's extraordinary complacency in the belief that the culture of scientists could solve most of the world's problems) complained that Snow's book "communicates the strongest possible wish that we should forget about politics."[19] Snow's book induced some defenders of the humanities to attack the culture of the sciences in harsh terms. But for the most part, instead of leveling charges against the sciences in general, these champions of the humanities attempted to chart the boundaries between the two worlds in the hope of clarifying what made one different from the other. No doubt many also hoped that defining these boundaries would help to gain recognition for the humanities' distinctive contribution to the national interest. In a sense, then, C.P. Snow's controversial book laid the groundwork for a national humanities foundation.

While many scholars in the humanities in the early 1960s were coming to think of themselves as belonging to a distinctive culture, many Americans were beginning to worry that the success of science might damage the social fabric of the nation. The critical skepticism of science, they argued, corroded traditional religious and moral values. No matter how necessary scientific research was to the defense of the nation or to the fight against disease, it was disturbing to see the sciences singled out for honor and support. Many writers insisted that America was too enamored of technology, too attached to scientific progress. In his autobiography, Norman Podhoretz voices what had become a common concern of the era: "I devoted a good deal of energy . . . to thinking and talking about how to 'humanize' industrial society."[20] Podhoretz had been joined by many political, civic, and industrial leaders, who worried that, as the *1964 Report* put it, "without really intending it, we are on the road toward becoming a dehumanized society."[21] In an editorial, the *New York Times* expressed the hope that "what the National Science Foundation has done for science and what the National Institutes of Health have done for medical research, the National Foundation on the Arts and Humanities . . . could also do [for the humanities]."[22]

If written five years or so earlier, the *1964 Report* probably would have sunk without a trace. But the climate of opinion had changed, and in 1964 many Americans were receptive to the idea that a national humanities foundation would foster what the report termed "humane values," values that were not in opposition to science but that would somehow keep science under control, would prevent the scientific outlook from dominating American life. Two months after the *1964 Report* was made public, Representative Moorhead declared, "In an age in which we have seen of necessity a spectacular growth in science, it is essential that we preserve the interdependence of science and the humanities, so that men will remain masters of their technology and not its unthinking servants."[23] It was a remark that many congressmen would repeat in the ensuing debate about a national humanities foundation.

When Moorhead cautioned that men should remain masters of their technology, he was borrowing from the language of the *1964 Report*, which consists of a short general essay, two appendixes, and a lengthy supplement. The prose of the main essay, which implies that the most important role of a national humanities foundation should be the diffusion of humanistic knowledge, is as fervid as it is imprecise. Declaring that "democracy demands wisdom of the average man," it asserts that a national humanities foundation would make us "wiser than we otherwise might be." Such a foundation would enable the average American to learn more about "such enduring values as justice, freedom, virtue, beauty, and truth," and to fulfill his need for humanistic "vision."[24]

By contrast, the prose of the appendixes and supplement is both more restrained and more precise. Of greater significance, the argument is somewhat different, for it is based on the assumption that a national humanities foundation would be concerned mainly with scholarly research and education in the humanities. One appendix concerns "The Humanities and the Schools," and the 160-page supplement consists of reports from twenty-four learned societies focusing mainly on the needs of scholars in the humanities. One general complaint runs like a refrain through most of the reports: owing to insufficient funds, scholars in the humanities are hampered in their research. Some of the reports also complain that the lack of money makes it difficult to recruit scholarly talent to the discipline. The report of the American Historical Association, for example, insists that "what the humanities need is better history; what society needs is better historians. We need to attract more men of ability into the profession."[25]

There is no question but that the proponents of a national humanities foundation were more concerned about the needs of scholars in the humanities than about the alleged need of the American public to be imbued with humanistic "vision." When the ACLS, an organization committed by its constitution to "the advancement of the humanistic studies in all fields of learning," took the initiative in establishing the Commission on the Humanities in 1963, it regarded NSF, which devotes the lion's share of its budget to the support of research, as an appropriate model for a national humanities foundation. Indeed, Charles Blitzer, staff director of the original commission, admitted that "in the 1960s, when we talked about a national humanities foundation, the model in our minds was clearly the National Science Foundation."[26] And in the Sponsor's Foreword to the *1964 Report*, the commission pointedly declared itself "mindful of the admirable record of the National Science Foundation"; it hoped a national humanities foundation would be governed and staffed by "men who enjoy the confidence of the scholarly community."[27]

If the commission wanted a national humanities foundation to be devoted primarily to the support of research in the humanities, why did it begin the *1964 Report* with an essay that makes so much of the need to diffuse the humanities? The answer must be political expediency. The commission probably assumed that Congress, less than enthusiastic about creating a new federal agency devoted mainly to research in the humanities, would be swayed by no other argument. Its report had to stress, as Keeney had stressed, that "we do not envisage the Foundation as entirely or even primarily an academic enterprise."[28]

Was Keeney being disingenuous? Probably not. Like the other members of the commission, he certainly envisioned a national humanities foundation supporting scholarly research, but, again like the rest of the commission, he vaguely hoped that the new agency could make some effort to reach the general public with programs in the humanities. The two choices of emphasis may reveal a certain confusion about how best to make a case for a national humanities foundation, a confusion that arose in part because, as Laurence Veysey has noted, the word humanities "is, surprisingly enough, an extreme latecomer in common American academic usage. In fact, the 1940s was the first decade when it had really wide resonance, the kind of resonance that would propel it toward eventual federal recognition in the National Endowment for the Humanities."[29] Because they were unsure of exactly what the humanities were—or indeed what they could do—the proponents of a national humanities foundation grasped at whatever argument they could.

But the success of the *1964 Report* may ultimately have had less to do with the main essay's strenuous argument in favor of diffusing the humanities than with the composition of the National Humanities Commission, whose distinguished membership included persons who were not closely associated with the humanities and therefore could not be accused of having axes to grind. Perhaps because men such as Thomas J. Watson, then chairman of IBM, and Glenn

T. Seaborg, chairman of the Atomic Energy Commission, served on the commission, the idea of a national humanities foundation became something it would be difficult for a legislator to make fun of without running the risk of being called a philistine—someone not sufficiently interested, as the *1964 Report* put it, in the nation's "social, moral, and aesthetic development."[30]

Thus in January 1965 a writer in *Science* noted that, "for better or worse, things have evolved in this country to the point where very few legislators dare make fun of what is considered to be intellectual activity."[31] And Robert Lumiansky, then president of the ACLS, could testify at the congressional hearings that the *1964 Report* "has been noted frequently and in detail in editorials, in newspaper and magazine articles, in important speeches, and the *Congressional Record*; the President of the United States has spoken of it favorably; numerous pertinent organizations have endorsed it by formal resolution; and . . . significantly, bills seeking to implement the Commission's report have been submitted with very strong sponsorship in both the Senate and the House of Representatives."[32]

Yet in one important way the *1964 Report* failed to bring the commission's recommendations to fruition. What Congress finally approved was not a national humanities foundation after all, but a National Foundation for the Arts and the Humanities consisting of two autonomous, equally funded divisions: the National Endowment for the Arts and the National Endowment for the Humanities. (Presumably the agencies were called endowments because they were authorized to accept private gifts, which would be matched, generally on a one-to-one basis, with funds coming not from their regular appropriations but from a special Treasury fund.) Both came under the supervision of a committee called the Federal Council on the Arts and the Humanities. Initially they shared an administrative staff, but eventually NEH and NEA became completely separate administrative entities.

Why were the agencies joined together in the first place? In the *1964 Report*, the commission recommended that support for the creative and performing arts be placed "within the scope" of a national humanities foundation, and at the congressional hearings both Keeney and Lumiansky urged that there be one foundation rather than two. "The arts and the humanities," Lumiansky reasoned, "are complementary aspects of a single enterprise, and in my view it would do them harm to separate them." Keeney testified that the commission had wrestled with the "fundamental question of whether or not the arts and humanities belonged together," deciding finally that "the arts are basically a major part of the substance of the humanities."[33]

The commission's conclusion was not only sensible, it was politically shrewd as well. The humanities stood to gain by being closely associated with the art world, which had already won several battles in its struggle to gain federal support. President Eisenhower had proposed in 1955 that Congress establish a Federal Advisory Commission on the Arts. No such legislation was enacted, and in 1961 President Kennedy's similar recommendation met the same fate. But the Kennedy administration was persistent: in 1962 August Heckscher was appointed special consultant on the arts, and a year later he issued a report, "The Arts and the National Government," which called for the establishment of a National Arts Foundation "on the model of the existing foundations in science and health."[34] The Senate soon passed a bill that closely followed the Heckscher report's recommendations, but it was killed in the House. Finally, in 1964 Congress passed the National Arts and Cultural Development Act, establishing a National Council on the Arts within the Executive Office of the President. With this enactment the arts at last gained long-sought federal recognition, if not yet actual federal support.

There was, however, a good chance that federal support for the arts would soon become a reality. In 1964 President Johnson declared that "history has shown that if we are to achieve the Great Society for which we are all working, it is essential that the arts grow and flourish."[35] And in his State of the Union address on January 5, 1965, he proposed a National Foundation on the Arts "to help promote and honor creative achievements." It was a proposal that Senator Jacob Javits of New York, a strong supporter of federal aid to the arts, found "electrifying."[36] Although four months earlier, in a speech at Brown University, Johnson had "look[ed] with the greatest of favor" on the commission's recommendation for a national humanities foundation,[37] he made no mention of the humanities in his State of the Union address. It was politically wise, therefore, for those testifying in behalf of a national humanities foundation to speak of the arts as closely related to, or even an essential component of, the humanities. If the arts managed to get through the door of federal funding, they might be able to drag the humanities through as well, or so members of the commission may have thought. According to Charles Blitzer, when the commission was formed the possibility that Congress would approve a national humanities foundation in the near future was considered remote.[38]

No doubt to the surprise of the commission, the political influence of the arts, greater than that of the humanities in 1964, waned after the publication of the *1964 Report* as the humanities quickly gained in political importance, perhaps becoming even more influential than the arts. Influence is difficult to gauge, but it was soon obvious to the proponents of a national arts foundation that they would need the support of those in favor of a similar foundation devoted to the humanities; their chances of success otherwise were slim. The difficulty lay in the House, which had killed President Kennedy's 1963 bill to establish a National Arts Foundation. There were fears that Johnson's proposal would suffer the same fate.

The arts and the humanities, then, needed each other in order to gain federal support, yet they were reluctant allies. Many of those at home in the world of the humanities had little in common with those who belonged to the world of the arts, and each world tended to regard the other with suspicion. Although the Commission on the Humanities spoke of the arts as "a major part of the substance of the humanities,"[39] it did not have a single performing or creative artist among its members. It is understandable, therefore, that supporters of the arts were worried that the sudden flurry of congressional interest in the humanities would lead to the creation of an agency in which the arts would be swallowed up by the humanities. The tension between the two worlds provoked Lumiansky to protest at the congressional hearings that "too much has been made during the last few months—and particularly since these hearings started—of the division, the suspicion, if you want to call it that, between the two entities, the arts and the humanities."[40]

Attempting to find a formula satisfactory to both parties, Frederick Burkhardt offered some politic advice. The arts and the humanities, he proposed, should be joined together in a single agency, but this agency should be made up of separate divisions, since the two disciplines "are very different, and require different kinds of training and expertise."[41] A number of congressmen, especially

Representative John Brademas of Indiana, had been thinking along these lines, for they were worried lest the arts not be given their due in a foundation devoted to the humanities. According to one report, Brademas was responsible for the language setting up the two separate endowments within the framework of a single agency, but it is probably more accurate to say that a number of persons hammered out the formula, having come to realize that it was the only one that would pass muster in Congress.[42] It was doubtful that Congress, especially the House, would support the creation of two new federal agencies, and it was equally doubtful that there was enough support in the House for the creation of an agency devoted exclusively to either the arts or the humanities.

In any case, the peculiar formula—one agency with two distinct divisions—was adopted by the Johnson administration, which on March 10 introduced a bill similar to that which Burkhardt had recommended. The administration's bill sailed through the Senate smoothly, provoking no deliberation whatsoever, but it encountered strong opposition in the House before it finally passed. The uneasy alliance between the arts and the humanities had paid off. Although yoked together in one agency, for all intents and purposes they were kept separate—which is probably what most proponents of a national humanities foundation had wanted despite all the testimony that the arts are essentially a branch of the humanities. Which world deserves the most credit for getting the legislation passed? It is impossible to say, but the members of the Commission on the Humanities must surely have realized that the arts connection had been invaluable.

Yet if its association with the arts had made NEH possible, in some ways the connection would prove to be a burden. NEH would continually be judged by how well it was doing in comparison with NEA, although the proponents of a national humanities foundation had never envisioned the work of such an agency being measured with an arts-foundation yardstick. "The proper sister of the humanities endowment is the National Science Foundation and not the National Endowment for the Arts," Charles Blitzer has said, adding that the comparison with NEA is inappropriate, since "the arts, by definition, presuppose an audience in a way that the humanities do not."[43]

For Blitzer and others, the legislative maneuvering that led to the twinning of NEA and NEH has been unfortunate in that it has led congressmen, and others as well, to assume that the primary mission of NEH is to gain a large public audience for the humanities rather than to improve the status of the humanities within academe. The shadow of NEA has always hovered over NEH, so much so that Joseph Duffey, chairman of NEH from 1977 to 1981, recently urged the task force appointed by President Reagan to "look carefully at and distinguish the work of the two Endowments. Both are important institutions. However, their areas of concern, their methods of operation—and their goals—differ."[44]

Yet it is not the arts connection alone that has encouraged Congress to believe NEH should be judged by the extent to which its programs have made an impact on the general public. After all, the opening essay of the *1964 Report* indicated that the agency's prime mission would be reaching the general public with programs in the humanities. If Americans embraced humanistic values, the *1964 Report* implied, they would have a more balanced outlook on life and would be less inclined toward mindless enthusiasm about material progress, technology, and science.

It is probable that many scholars in the humanities paid little attention to the opening essay of the *1964 Report*, assuming that it was for public and congressional consumption. Yet some were concerned about a number of assumptions that underlay not only that essay but other defenses of the humanities. Some scholars, for example, were strongly critical of the notion that the humanities are purveyors of values, agreeing with historian Joseph Strayer that "there are no 'values' inherent in the humanities."[45] Some, indeed, felt, as John Higham did, that "there has never been the slightest agreement about the proper role of values in any field."

Some also worried that the creation of an agency devoted to the humanities would reinforce distinctions between the humanities, social sciences, and natural sciences that were no longer meaningful. Writing in 1966, the year NEH began its operations, Higham observed: "The humanities as we know them today in America comprise no meaningful or coherent entity. To conceive of them still as distinct from the social sciences in the exercise of qualitative judgment is to perpetuate stereotypes colored by the dislocations of a generation ago." Higham also wondered if it were "possible that the 'humanists' have at last achieved official recognition in America at the very moment when the antagonistic confrontation of the two cultures is beginning to yield to new unities and new diversities." He implied that the victory "humanists" had gained in attaining federal recognition for their work might be Pyrrhic in the sense that it would tend to perpetuate outmoded distinctions, and noted that "it is by no means easy to say what is science and what is 'merely' humanistic."[46]

In addition, some scientists were worried that the creation of NEH might set up an unnatural boundary between the sciences and the humanities. In a letter of support for a national humanities foundation, Leland Haworth, the director of NSF, attacked the "common habit of drawing a hard and fast line between the humanities and the sciences." Although generally approving of federal support for the humanities, Haworth was disturbed by those who spoke glibly of humanistic or humane values, thereby implying that the sciences were inhumane. Science, Haworth contended, "is not inhumane, and it is easily demonstrated that the life of the human race has been enriched by the idea of science, as well as by the material benefits which science has made possible."[47]

But these concerns, especially on the part of those within the humanities community, should not be exaggerated. By and large, scholars in the humanities were delighted to have an agency they could call their own, and if they were uncomfortable with the ringing phrases of the *1964 Report*'s opening essay, they took it for granted that such rhetoric was necessary in order to impress upon Congress the need for a national humanities foundation, and that it would have little effect on the actual work of the agency. Surely the agency would allocate its funds based on the judgments of distinguished professional scholars—historians, literary critics, philosophers—and would not be preoccupied with defining the humanities, for the term was nothing more than a convenient rubric under which a variety of disciplines congregated. While the creation of only one federal agency devoted to supporting the arts, the humanities, and the sciences, along the lines suggested by Lumiansky at the congressional hearings, would have been preferable, that idea was politically inexpedient (or so at least it seemed at the time), so it made sense to have a national humanities foundation to support research in disciplines that NSF considered outside its purview.[48]

Yet if most scholars in the humanities paid little attention to the opening essay of the *1964 Report*, many congressmen were impressed with it. They spoke of a "national crisis" and a "dangerous imbalance" if federal support for the humanities was not forthcoming. In the Senate, where the administration's bill passed quickly, many were fervent in its praise. Senator Ralph Yarborough of Texas acclaimed its passage as "a sign that American culture, far from standing still, is pressing forward toward her appointed rendezvous with a golden age."[49] Yarborough's enthusiastic endorsement of the new agency, applauded in the Senate by Republicans as well as Democrats, was matched by that of many congressmen in the House. Perhaps the most ardent approval came from Representative Claude Pepper of Florida, who declared that "active attention to the humanities and arts is necessary for the welfare and happiness of America and mankind," adding that the measure would provide "relief to meet the fundamental needs of our people" as well as to "purify, beautify, and . . . strengthen the soul of America."[50]

These proclamations of faith cannot, of course, be taken at face value as signs that either the *1964 Report* or the testimony at the congressional hearings had truly won most of Congress over to the cause of federal support for the arts and the humanities. Since there was no organized public opposition to the administration's bill, and since the appropriations being recommended were only $5 million for each endowment for three years, supporting it was a risk-free way for congressmen to express concern for the nation's health without fear of being accused of fiscal extravagance. But while it is doubtful that many congressmen were as interested in federal support for the arts and the humanities as they claimed to be, it is probably true that many thought it was vaguely in the national interest to make some gesture of recognition toward the arts and the humanities. And with only one exception, even those who opposed the bill were careful to say that they, too, hoped that the arts and the humanities would flourish in the United States.

The exception is worthy of note, if only because it probably made congressional opposition to the bill even more difficult. Calling the measure a boondoggle, Representative H.R. Gross of Iowa attempted to puncture his colleagues' many defenses of the bill in a deliberately outrageous attack. At one point Gross offered an amendment that would have expanded the scope of arts activities to include belly dancing, baseball, football, golf, tennis, squash, pinochle, and poker.[51]

Needless to say, other critics of the bill were more restrained. Seven out of ten Republicans on the House Committee on Education and Labor, the committee in charge of the bill, issued a minority report in which they charged that the committee's handling of the bill was "hasty and frivolous" and made a "mockery of the legislative process." Even Representative Ogden Reid of New York, who supported the bill, admitted that it had gone through the committee "at a very rapid rate—roughly, fifteen minutes." The result of this "railroading," as the minority report called it, was a poorly-thought-out piece of legislation, one that would create "an impenetrable thicket of duplication and overlapping." Contending that such a "formidable bureaucratic network" would be a clumsy way of supporting the arts and the humanities, the minority report recommended that the bill be sent back to the committee so that other ways of supporting the arts and the humanities—for example, with tax reforms—could be considered.[52]

The bill's opponents also claimed that the creation of two endowments would be detrimental to both the arts and the humanities. "We are considering a bill that not only defies clear and precise understanding," Representative Robert B. Duncan of Oregon protested, "but which tends to defeat one of its own objectives—the support and encouragement of artistic excellence."[53] Opponents believed that, far from stimulating the arts and the humanities, the bill would actually stifle them as the "deadening hand of the federal bureaucracy" (in the words of the House Republican Committee) led to "attempts at the political control of culture."[54] Arguing that the passage of the bill would place "a federal straitjacket over creativity," Representative William S. Broomfield of Michigan warned that "things being what they are in Washington, we can be sure that if this bill is passed, the day will not be far off before we demand political allegiance of those who receive federal gifts, that we see the controversial ignored and the mediocre praised."[55] Broomfield's fears, which focused on the arts rather than the humanities, were shared by many opponents of the bill, some of them Democrats. There were writers and artists, too, who were dubious about federal support of culture, and Representative Robert Griffin of Michigan quoted the essayist and critic Russell Lynes, who contended that "the less the arts have to do with our political processes . . . the healthier they will be."[56]

The proponents of federal support for the arts and the humanities, however, had taken such concerns into account, for the authorizing legislation made it clear that the two endowments were to be essentially passive creatures, receiving applications that would be judged primarily on the basis of peer review. The reviewers, none of them employees of the government, would make recommendations to a national council—a body that would presumably not be swayed by partisan considerations—composed of twenty-six presidential appointees, many of whom would be scholars in the humanities. Final grant-making authority would repose in the chairmen of the endowments. In the House there was some debate as to whether the chairmen should have such authority, but it was pointed out that it would be exceedingly difficult for the chairmen to oppose the advice of the national council without incurring the suspicion that they were acting politically. And if the structure of the endowments made it unlikely that they would become politicized, so too would their low level of appropriations ensure that they would not play a major role in American culture.

To say that the fears of NEH's opponents were exaggerated is not to say that they were unfounded. The specter of political control of culture may have been merely a fantasy, but concern that the endowments might be deflected from their mandate was legitimate for a number of reasons. The desire to fund projects that appealed to certain influential congressmen or certain important institutions in the humanities, the desire to make grants that would gain the agency a good deal of publicity, and, most importantly, the desire to distribute funds as widely as possible to placate congressmen who feared their districts or states were gaining less than their fair share of grants—all of these possibilities made reasonable the concern that, in the long run, narrowly political considerations would loom large in the review process.

The opponents of the bill were even more convincing when they raised the question of need, an issue unfortunately confused by the fact that the needs of the arts and those of the humanities were quite different. According to a 1965 report by the Rockefeller Brothers Fund, the needs of the arts were clear: the costs of running symphony orchestras, ballet companies, or operas, all labor-intensive enterprises, were prohibitive and could not be met by ticket sales, barring dramatic price increases, which would make cultural programming the exclusive preserve of the rich. The report advocated a major expansion of federal, state, and local support for the arts. According to the Commission on the Humanities, however, entirely different needs plagued the humanistic disciplines. They were suffering a brain drain; the best minds were going into science because science was more lucrative. Moreover, the best scholars in the humanities, unlike those in the sciences, had little time off to do research, and there were very few grants available.

The main argument for federal support of the humanities, then, centered on the notion of imbalance—an imbalance that was depleting the ranks of potential scholars and teachers in the humanistic disciplines. "We are finding," Lumiansky declared, "a tremendous scarcity of properly prepared teachers to do the teaching and to do the advanced work necessary." Virtually every witness at the congressional hearings stressed this same point. According to Representative Dante St. Germain of Rhode Island, "Many of our potentially brilliant students in the arts and the humanities have elected to follow other career fields in which the rewards and recognition could be considered more sure."[57] He echoed the findings of the *1964 Report* that the "American practitioners of the humanities— the professionals, so to speak—are now prevented in certain specific ways from realizing their full capacities and from attracting enough first-rate individuals into their ranks," and that, in consequence, "in the colleges and universities there is a great need for graduate scholarships and fellowships for the preliminary training of scholars, teachers, and artists at all stages. . . ." An essay in *Science* declared that the needs of the humanities were clear.[58]

Actually, these needs were far from clear. True, in the early 1960s the academic world was short of teachers in the humanities, but the shortage was the result of tremendous increases in college enrollments in general and in humanities courses in particular. Even Lumiansky admitted that "the areas we are interested in are experiencing a kind of boom." The *Wall Street Journal* reported in April 1965 that "since 1957—the year Russia's first Sputnik roared into space and the big push for more scientists got under way in the United States—the annual number of college graduates with degrees in the humanities and social sciences has soared more than 50 percent, to more than 376,000. . . . In the same span, the total of science graduates has risen less than 30 percent, to not quite 126,000 a year."[59] Temporarily, the supply of teachers of the humanities had been insufficient to meet demand. But this need was being met very quickly. Indeed, by the end of the 1960s supply would exceed demand, and by the end of the 1970s there would be a vast oversupply of teachers of the humanities to a point at which, according to a 1980 Carnegie Council Report, only one out of ten holders of new doctorates in English or in foreign languages would secure a tenured position.[60]

Why had the commission offered such a misguided analysis of trends in the teaching profession? For one thing, it had paid no attention to demographic studies showing college enrollments leveling off by the early 1970s and possibly even declining by the late 1970s. In the summer of 1965, for instance, an observer in the *Educational Record* warned that there would soon be too few college students to afford employment to all the Ph.D.'s emerging from the nation's flourishing graduate programs.[61] Second, the commission had failed to heed the dynamics of the marketplace. It was precisely the temporary shortage of teachers of the humanities that made a career as a scholar-teacher so attractive. Since the demand for highly regarded potential scholars was much greater than the supply, the best young people entering the profession usually had numerous jobs from which to choose—jobs that paid relatively well and involved relatively light teaching loads. Moreover, most of these jobs led to tenure in six years.

Thus, it was untrue that federal money was needed to attract young men and women to careers in the humanistic disciplines. No doubt scholars in the humanities were not as well paid as scientists; no doubt fewer grants were available to them than to scientists. Nevertheless, the 1960s were a golden age of affluence and mobility for scholars in the humanities, an age that bore little resemblance to the one adumbrated by the commission. If there was a brain drain, it was away from the sciences and into the humanities; enrollment for advanced degrees in the humanities increased much more dramatically in the 1960s than enrollment for similar degrees in the sciences. The figures speak for themselves: in 1960, 37,185 persons enrolled for advanced degrees in the humanities (excluding history); in 1969 the figure was 99,510. By contrast, in 1960, 25,707 persons enrolled for advanced degrees in the physical sciences (excluding mathematics); in 1969 the figure was 39,885.[62]

On the question of manpower, then, Representative Durward G. Hall of Missouri was correct in insisting that there was "no demonstrated need" for the proposed bill. His colleague Paul Findley of Illinois argued that a more pressing need was for federal belt-tightening, since the government was $8 billion in debt. Findley also questioned the alleged crisis in the humanities, citing the article in the *Wall Street Journal* as evidence.[63] Led by the likes of Hall and Findley, a fairly stiff challenge, including a motion by Representative Griffin to recommit (in effect, to kill) the bill, was mounted in the House by its opponents.

The bill's proponents prevailed, yet their arguments had been based to some extent on misguided assumptions and questionable evidence. In the mid-1960s it was far from obvious what the needs of the humanities were. Perhaps a national humanities foundation was needed only in the sense implied by Frederick Burkhardt, who remarked at the congressional hearings that what was needed "perhaps above all else . . . [is] an expression of national concern and regard for the work of humanists."[64] A national humanities foundation would give the culture of the humanities what the culture of the sciences had already gained: recognition and respect. Its founding would signal to Americans that the health of the humanities was important to the nation, if not so obviously important as the health of the sciences.

James Madison, in a letter written in 1822, had declared:

The American people owe it to themselves, and to the cause of free Government, to prove by their establishments for the advancement and diffusion of Knowledge, that their political Institutions, which are attracting observation from every quarter, and are respected as Models, by the new-born States in our own Hemisphere, are as favorable to the intellectual and moral improvement of Man as they are conformable to his individual & social Rights. What spectacle can be more edifying or more seasonable, than that of Liberty & Learning, each leaning on the other for their mutual & surest support?[65]

Madison never called specifically for a national humanities foundation, but—like Hamilton, Washington, Jefferson, and Adams—he did favor the idea of a national university to be supported with federal funds. All the founding fathers had argued that, since an enlightened citizenry was necessary to ensure the stability of a republican form of government, the national and state governments should find ways to foster such enlightenment.

Perhaps the Congress in 1965 had, to some degree at least, done the right thing for the wrong reasons. Surely it was appropriate to establish NEH, for a great nation should honor and promote achievement in both the sciences and the humanities. But those who lobbied for a national humanities foundation did not speak so much of the connection between learning and liberty as they did of the values of the humanistic disciplines and the needs of scholars in those disciplines. They also, as we have seen, promised what could never be delivered: a large public audience for the humanities. The result of that promise was that many people—among them Senator Pell, later to wield a good deal of influence over NEH—expected NEH to resemble NEA, not NSF. And Pell's understanding of NEH's mandate was to shape the way in which the agency developed during the 1970s.

2

A Short History
of the Endowment

LIKE THE National Science Foundation and the National Endowment for the Arts, the National Endowment for the Humanities is primarily a grant-making agency. It devises categories of support and invites individuals or institutions (depending upon the nature of the category) to apply for grants in particular categories. The applications undergo peer review, a process in which grant applications are evaluated by specialists in their respective fields rather than by employees of the agency, although the agency itself makes the final decisions on the awarding of grant monies. NEA and NEH are both, in a sense, indirect patrons of the arts and the humanities, since they assign major roles in the award-giving process to independent artists and scholars. This procedure is by no means standard for government agencies, many of which operate in a different manner: they award contracts rather than grants, deciding exactly what kind of work they want done and then inviting individuals or organizations to submit proposals to do it.

NEH and NEA were organized along the lines of NSF in order to allay fears that collectively they might become a sort of ministry of culture, high-handedly deciding what the country needed in the arts and humanities areas or, even worse, awarding contracts in response to lobbying or to repay political favors. The peer review process—which, as we shall see in chapter 4, differs somewhat in the three agencies—fosters independent evaluation, yet we should keep in mind that the chairmen and staff of NEH and NEA not only choose reviewers, they also design the particular categories to be supported and make recommendations to Congress about the level of funding for each category. The agencies, then, are far from passive mechanisms simply receiving proposals for funding, assigning them to independent scholars or artists for review, and taking action on the basis of reviewers' recommendations.

When NEH began operations in 1966 it was unclear just what categories of support would best enable it to carry out the directions of its authorizing legislation to "develop and encourage the pursuit of a national policy for the promotion of progress and scholarship in the humanities." The agency's *Second Annual Report* noted that "the legislative mandate of the Humanities Endowment is sufficiently broad, and the humanities themselves are so diversified, that the chief task of the past fiscal year has been to identify areas of greatest need, and to develop methods of supporting them."[1]

Although burdened with "identify[ing] areas of greatest need," the fledgling agency could thank Congress for relieving it of the task of defining what was meant by the humanities, for the enabling legislation spelled out the disciplines involved. The humanities, it said, "includes, but is not limited to, the study of the following: language, both modern and classical; linguistics; literature; history; jurisprudence; philosophy; archeology; the history, criticism, and theory of the arts; and those aspects of the social sciences which have humanistic content and employ humanistic methods." In 1968 Congress added the phrase "and the study and application of the humanities to the human environment," to which it appended in 1970, "with particular attention to the relevance of the humanities to the current conditions of national life." In 1970 Congress also added comparative religion and ethics to the list of disciplines encompassed by the humanities.

The definition poses some obvious problems of interpretation. What, for instance, is the meaning of the phrase "includes, but is not limited to, the study of the following . . ."? What precisely is meant by the question-begging phrase "those aspects of the social sciences which have humanistic content and employ humanistic methods"? Yet it would be a mistake to make too much of these obfuscations, for the definitions did make it possible for NEH to avoid becoming bogged down in its infancy in internal debate about what is meant by the humanities. Congress also had the foresight to spell out in broad terms what kinds of activities it expected NEH to pursue: (1) to "initiate and support research and programs to strengthen the research potential of the United States in the humanities" (the phrase "research potential" was amended in 1973 to "research and teaching potential"); (2) to "award fellowships and grants to institutions or individuals for training and workshops in the humanities"; and (3) to "foster, through grants or other arrangements with groups, public understanding and appreciation of the humanities." In short, the agency was asked to support research, teaching, and public programs in the humanities. In order to do so it set up three main divisions: Fellowships, Research and Publications, and Education and Special Projects. Later, in 1969, the Division of Education and Special Projects would be divided into the Division of Education and the Division of Public Programs.

By and large, NEH has remained faithful to these categories of support. Although each chairman has tried to make his term of office distinctive, there has been a good deal of continuity in the agency's programs and procedures. But the most significant fact about the first five years of the agency's existence is that its budget grew very slowly—from $2.5 million in program funds in 1966 (expended in 1967 because 1966 was devoted mainly to planning) to $6.05 million in 1970. During the first five years, moreover, by far the largest part of NEH's funding—80 percent, for instance, in 1968—went toward research.

The imbalance in allocations to research and public programs was not exactly what NEH had originally intended. Barnaby Keeney, a historian and president of Brown University who was selected by President Johnson to head NEH, stated in the Endowment's *First Annual Report* that "the agency's most challenging opportunity [is] to increase the interest in and use of the humanities by our citizens, and to improve their access to them."[2] The new agency, Keeney believed, would be judged in Congress mainly on the extent to which its programs reached a broad public, rather than on how well it served the scholarly community. But it proved difficult for NEH in its infancy to spend money on public programs in the humanities, for the agency was venturing into uncharted territory. The *Fourth Annual Report* acknowledged that "a good deal of time has been given, within the Endowment and within the National Council on the Humanities, to the question of exactly how it [reaching the public with programs in the humanities] should be done."[3] There was no obvious audience for such programs, nor was there an obvious pool of applicants willing to develop them. It was not difficult for NEH to award research funds, since innumerable scholars were eager to apply for research grants. But who would apply for grants to develop public programs in the humanities?

NEH was thus obliged in its early years to take an active role in searching for individuals and organizations capable of creating public programs. Moreover, the agency found it had to work closely with these applicants as they prepared their proposals, in order to ensure that a significant percentage would pass muster with independent reviewers. As a result of these efforts the agency's level of support for public programs had increased by 1970; in that year 16 percent of its funds were expended on public programs, as compared to only 10 percent in 1967. But NEH had a long way to go before Congress would be pleased with its efforts.

In its early years NEH tried to ensure the continued good will of Congress by stressing the relevance of the humanities to contemporary political problems. Indeed, its *Third Annual Report* declared the agency ready to "give priority in its grant-making to proposals for studies related to contemporary problems."[4] The National Council defined specific areas of concern in encouraging "appropriate project proposals within the various fields of the humanities as they bear on urbanization, minority problems, war, peace, and foreign policy; problems of Governmental decision, civil liberties and the wider application of humanistic knowledge and insights to the general public interest."[5]

What effect did this shopping list have on the actual workings of the agency? NEH betrayed its uneasiness about the National Council's agenda in its *Fifth Annual Report*, declaring: "Few statements so brief raise such imposing questions of implementation."[6] Reviewers of applications were not directed to give extra points to proposals focusing on urbanization, minority problems, war, peace, and so on. Indeed, the National Council had stressed that "each proposal, regardless of its emphasis . . . will be judged primarily on its intrinsic merit."[7] So it is doubtful that such proposals fared better than others in the peer review process. NEH, then, did not exactly rally 'round the flag of relevance, and in the *Fourth Annual Report* Keeney himself remarked that the agency's emphasis on relevance "has not blinded it to the value of basic research, which Congress and the public now understand so well concerning the sciences."[8] If the sciences are awarded money for "pure" scientific research, Keeney implied, why should the humanities not be funded for "pure" humanistic research?

If Keeney was at best lukewarm about the idea that NEH should be particularly concerned with social issues and problems of public policy, Ronald Berman, who became chairman late in 1971, was downright leery of the notion. Berman, a professor of English at the University of California at San Diego and the author of *America in the Sixties: An Intellectual History*, made this evident in his Foreword to the *Seventh Annual Report*: "There are many social issues in which the Endowment does not believe itself obliged to participate. The most liberal definition of the humanities' interests must necessarily exclude the determination of public policy or the various forms of social advocacy."[9]

Under Berman's chairmanship, however, the Endowment did tacitly endorse the notion that the humanities can help to clarify, if not actually to solve, questions of public policy, since the state humanities committees, which were formed in 1971 before Berman came to NEH, were required to support projects focusing on public policy. By 1975 there were such committees in all fifty states, and in 1976 Congress stipulated that at least 20 percent of NEH's program funds be divided among these state committees. (In 1977 the state committees became the responsibility of a separate division of NEH, State Programs.) Because many of the state humanities committees found the public-policy requirement onerous, it was dropped in 1977. Nevertheless, as a recent NEH brochure demonstrates, state committees are still urged to "concentrate their efforts on projects which relate the humanities to matters of broad public interest and affect public policy."[10]

Under Berman's chairmanship, which lasted until 1976, the agency saw a steady growth in the percentage of its funds expended for public programs—from 18 percent in 1971 to 38 percent in 1976. But what was most striking about the Berman incumbency was the dramatic growth of NEH's budget. In 1971 the agency received $11.1 million in program funds; by 1976 the amount had leaped to $72 million. Program funds, however, do not tell the whole story, for NEH maintains another, separate account with the federal government for so-called gift and matching funds, and uses monies from this second account to match private gifts for particular projects.

Proposals that include promises of private support must go through the normal review process, but if funding is approved they may receive a combination of both program (or "outright") funds and gift and matching funds. In 1971 NEH's gift and matching funds authorization was $2.5 million; by 1976 it had jumped to $7.5 million, of which all but $1 million was used.

Also under Berman's chairmanship NEH drew up a shopping list of desirable proposals, calling for applications focusing on the "American experience in its broadest sense." In 1973 the National Council had suggested that the upcoming Bicentennial should provide a major focus for NEH programs through the next three years; and the agency itself, in its *Eighth Annual Report*, exhorted applicants: "Since a serious recognition of the Bicentennial will require just the kind of intelligent nationwide exploration of America that the Endowment was created by Congress to foster, NEH . . . encourages the submission of applications for projects which bring the humanities to bear on serious study of the American experience from colonial times to the present, with particular—but not exclusive—emphasis on the period surrounding the founding of the nation."[11]

Was the encouragement of projects focusing on "the American experience" perhaps less a serious expression of intent than an attempt to persuade Congress that NEH was not primarily devoted to supporting esoteric scholarship in the humanities? This was apparently so, since the *Eighth Annual Report* was at pains to make clear that "any Bicentennial activities supported by the Endowment . . . will be extensions of its customary activities and conducted through the usual processes of the Endowment."[12] The agency's expression of interest in Bicentennial projects did, however, translate itself into a new category of support: the Bicentennial Histories Program, administered by the Research Division. In 1974 this division organized the State, Local, and Regional Studies Program, obviously restricted to proposals centering on American history. This is not to say that the call for applications on American themes constituted a significant change of direction for the agency. NEH had always been interested in supporting projects on American history and culture, a concern reflected in its considerable support for projects such as editing the works of leading American writers and political figures.

Joseph Duffey replaced Berman at the helm of NEH in 1977. A

former college professor and official of the American Association of University Professors, Duffey had played an important part in Jimmy Carter's successful presidential campaign. He had run Carter's Washington office and, before being appointed to the chairmanship of NEH, had been Carter's assistant secretary of state for educational and cultural affairs. Under Duffey the Public Programs Division continued to grow, its share of the agency's program funds increasing from 14 percent in 1976 to 21 percent in 1980. The increase was partially offset by a decrease in the percentage of funds allocated to State Programs, from 24 percent in 1976 to 21 percent in 1980, but the total amount allocated to public programming was more than 42 percent thanks to the creation in 1979 of a new division, Special Programs. Into the new department went two categories of support formerly housed within Public Programs: Program Development, which funded projects involving labor unions, ethnic groups, and national adult membership organizations; and Special Projects, a catch-all category devised to support projects that forged direct links between scholarly research and national audiences. Broadly speaking, then, in 1980 approximately 50 percent of NEH's funds were being allocated to categories of support that funded programs for the benefit of the general public.

Under Duffey's chairmanship the rate of increase in the agency's appropriations declined, although its actual budget increased, rising to $106.5 million in 1981. This figure does not take into account a new program begun in 1977—Challenge Grants. Designed to provide operational support for institutions connected with the humanities, these grants constitute a fund-raising mechanism to enable such institutions to "broaden their bases of individual and corporate support by offering one Federal dollar to match at least three non-federal dollars raised by the institution, either from new sources or from increases beyond the regular contributions of traditional sources."[13] Challenge Grants make up a third category of NEH funds, separate from both program funds and gift and matching funds. Monies from the new category are intended "to improve an institution's financial base, administration, and managerial structure, so that it will be able to perform its functions in the humanities."[14] Challenge Grants is the most significant new program developed by the agency since its inception, for no other NEH program offers general support for institutions in the humanities. In 1981 NEH made

$24 million available for Challenge Grants, out of a total budget for the year (including administrative costs) of $151.3 million.

Under Duffey a new shopping list for proposals was drawn up. At a congressional hearing, the chairman announced that NEH was "highlighting" American social history because it was an area of "clear and definite need." Projects involving folklore as well as technology and human values were also being funded, but the main emphasis during Duffey's years as chairman was clearly on social history. What Duffey called a "social history initiative" was a priority across all program areas.[15] It is not altogether clear what Duffey meant by this "initiative," since reviewers were not asked to give special weight to proposals in social history.

If the different programmatic emphases of Keeney, Berman, and Duffey had little effect on the disbursement of the agency's funds, what impact does the chairman have on the work of NEH? That depends in part on the role the chairman himself decides to play. When William J. Bennett became chairman of NEH early in 1982, he made it clear that he would play a very active role. A scholar of American political philosophy and constitutional law, with a law degree and a doctorate in philosophy, Bennett had previously been president of the National Humanities Center, a private institute for humanistic research in North Carolina. Soon after taking office at NEH he voiced his displeasure with a film focusing on the current regime in Nicaragua, funded by the Wisconsin Committee for the Humanities, declaring that "neither its theme nor its approach was related to the humanities."[16] He also let it be known that he would not necessarily support projects recommended by peer reviewers and the National Council. "I am not going to sign what I can't defend or what I think can't be defended by someone else with some persuasion."[17] Although a *New York Times* article suggested that Bennett would be stressing noncontroversial educational projects,[18] Bennett established anything but a low profile for himself. He began speaking out on a variety of questions, most notably on the importance of solid humanities courses in schools and colleges, and announced that NEH would begin a series of summer seminars for high-school teachers in which participants would read great books rather than devise new curricula or teaching methods.

The chairman does make a difference to NEH—more of a difference in some areas than in others. The peer review process, for instance, limits his role, since if he rejects the recommendations of peer reviewers and the National Council too often, he will arouse both controversy and resentment. In general, the world of scholarship, where continuing debate takes place (for the most part) within the confines of particular disciplines and follows its course regardless of NEH policy, is indifferent to his pronouncements. But many people in the world of education and public programs—deans, department chairmen, filmmakers, curators—pay close attention to the chairman of NEH, if only to get some idea of the kinds of proposals the agency is likely to look upon with favor.

In budgetary matters, however, the chairman's role is limited. Although he is not, strictly speaking, a member of any administration, since he is appointed for a specific term of office and cannot be fired by the president, a chairman would find it difficult to oppose the budget assigned to him by the administration that nominated him for office. And he must of course abide by the budget appropriated him by Congress. During the first fifteen years of NEH's existence, differences over the agency's budget rarely arose between the White House, the chairman of NEH, and Capitol Hill, since there was a general consensus that NEH should receive more funds. Some observers felt the rate of increase was insufficient to meet the needs of the humanities, but in fact NEH was one of the fastest-growing agencies in Washington, awarding 653 grants to 2,942 applicants in 1971 at a cost of $14.2 million, compared to 2,632 grants to 7,882 applicants in 1981 in the amount (up almost tenfold) of $140 million.

In 1982, however, applications declined to 6,964, perhaps because many would-be applicants thought NEH's budget had been cut dramatically and that their chances of getting a grant were therefore slim. The Reagan administration did argue for arts and humanities cutbacks of approximately 50 percent, but it found itself immediately at odds with Congress over the budgets of both NEH and NEA. Bennett, who was appointed by the Reagan administration and who was a self-proclaimed Reagan supporter, strongly defended the White House's budget for NEH, declaring himself the first NEH chairman with "the responsibility and inclination to defend a smaller budget." Although in 1981 and 1982 Congress rejected the administration's requests, cutting NEH's budget by only $21 million instead of the $55 million the administration had proposed, Bennett implied that he might not spend all the funds appropriated. "You can be sure," he said, "that if we can't spend it responsibly, we won't."[19]

Bennett claimed that a smaller budget would lead to a more efficient agency, an agency that would support only high-quality projects. Funding, he said, would be allotted according to "raised standards of evaluation," with "quality our main concern."[20] Many observers, to whom it appeared that NEH was being singled out by the Reagan administration for excessive budget cuts, were skeptical of Bennett's reasoning. In June 1983 the House subcommittee responsible for NEH's appropriations recommended a budget of $150 million for NEH, 30 percent higher than the Reagan administration's request. If NEH receives this much, Bennett said, "we either get more excellent applications or we look again at the possibility of . . . other new ventures for projects."[21] Despite Bennett's objections, it seemed likely that Congress would give NEH more than it asked for. But if NEH's budget might well increase during the remainder of the 1980s, it seemed unlikely to increase substantially. NEH's days of dramatic expansion were over.

3

The Politics of NEH

IN 1981 approximately half of NEH's budget (excluding its operating costs and challenge grants) was expended on public programs in the humanities; the proportion had been even higher in the late 1970s. In this respect NEH stands in striking contrast to its early model, the National Science Foundation, which in recent years has spent less than 1 percent of its budget on similar programs in the sciences. Why has NEH devoted so much of its budget to benefit the American public? And why, toward the end of the 1970s, did it begin to cut back on its support of public programs? To find answers to these questions we must take a close look at the politics of NEH.

After receiving scant attention from the press during the first ten years of its existence, NEH became newsworthy in 1976 and 1977. One reason was Senator Pell's vociferous opposition to the reappointment of Ronald Berman (chairman of the agency since late 1971), which resulted in a good deal of comment on the nature of Pell's objections and on Berman's record as chairman. A second reason was the controversial appointment in 1977 of Joseph Duffey to the chairmanship after a protracted and well publicized search on the part of the Carter administration. NEH—and to a lesser degree the National Endowment for the Arts—had become topics of frequent discussion, and the policies the two agencies might follow under new leadership were matters of widespread concern. Soon after Duffey's appointment to NEH and the appointment of Livingston Biddle, a former aide to Senator Pell, to the chairmanship of NEA, Hilton Kramer, writing in the *New York Times,* warned that "a spectre is haunting the arts and the humanities in the United States today . . . the spectre of a catastrophic shift of government policy in cultural affairs." Kramer and others were afraid that, as

Kramer put it, "a new era marked by an aggressive politicization of federal cultural policy is now imminent."[1]

Kramer was at pains to make very clear just what he meant by politicization. He spoke of the "crass political manner in which the Carter White House made its appointments of the endowment chairmanships," both of which, he said, "bear the stigma of cynical political convenience."[2] Duffey and Biddle, he implied, would act less as spokesmen for the humanities and the arts than as spokesmen for the Carter administration, and the endowments would henceforth let political considerations play an important part in the awarding of grants.

Kramer's apprehensions were heightened by a White House memorandum stating that "the Endowments' most important initiatives will almost certainly be in non-traditional and public areas."[3] According to Kramer, this ill-considered shift in emphasis would mean that "numbers—rather than quality, knowledge or distinction—[would become] the touchstone of achievement." Indeed, NEH might turn into a "political pork barrel."[4] Even those who defended Duffey's appointment were unhappy about the possibility of a shift in NEH policy. In a letter to the *New York Times,* William Phillips, the editor of the *Partisan Review,* wrote that "unless the criterion of quality is applied in each instance, we will have created an enormous pork barrel for the arts and the humanities."[5]

The concerns of Kramer and others about what might happen to NEH were understandable, for although Duffey had at one time been a teacher of the humanities he had been nominated for the chairmanship primarily as a result of the active part he had played in Carter's presidential campaign. True, former chairman Berman had been a Republican, but Berman had not been active in politics, and his credentials as a scholar of the humanities had been more impressive than Duffey's. Moreover, Duffey's wife, Anne Wexler, was a close associate of Carter's and was soon to become an important aide in the Carter White House.

What Kramer and other worried observers failed to realize was that the Carter administration's view of NEH closely resembled Congress's long-standing view of the agency. Duffey made it clear that NEH under his leadership would try to find ways of awarding a greater percentage of grants to minorities, but Congress had always been interested in funding "non-traditional and public areas,"

increasing the number of members of the general public benefiting
from programs supported by NEH, and establishing as wide as possible a geographical distribution of grants—precisely the kinds of
effort implicit in Duffey's policies. Certainly there were differences
between Carter and erstwhile chairman Berman, but by focusing on
these differences observers ignored the obvious fact that it was Congress that had been the major force in shaping NEH. And the single
most important figure affecting NEH and NEA in Congress was
plainly Senator Pell, who for fifteen years reigned as chairman of
the Senate subcommittee responsible for the continued reauthorization of the National Foundation for the Arts and the Humanities.

Perhaps because he was instrumental in the founding of NEH,
Senator Pell has always regarded the agency as his special responsibility. Other congressmen have also played supporting roles in
shaping NEH, but congressional courtesy, and perhaps congressional indifference as well, have enabled Pell to assert himself not
only as the "father of the humanities endowment"[6] but also as its
long-term champion. Pell himself told Berman in 1975 that "I have
followed this activity with the sense of parenthood for many more
years than you have."[7] To a large extent Senator Pell's views about
the agency's development have gone unchallenged by other senators.

Pell's interest in NEH and NEA was hardly the result of pressures
from his constituents. His support for the endowments arose instead
out of a strong personal conviction that both agencies were needed
to improve "the quality of American life."[8] But Pell has apparently
felt all along that NEH has had less impact on American life than
NEA because it has remained too close to academe. In 1970, concerned about the small percentage of NEH grants going "to what
are called the street-corner humanists as opposed to the Ph.D. humanists," he urged Barnaby Keeney to expand NEH's programs for
the general public, in part by establishing a state humanities program on the model of the already existing state arts councils. "It is
one of my ardent hopes," he told Keeney, "that your programs will
have more of an impact on the general population."[9]

Although NEH's support for public programs increased dramatically during the next five years, Pell remained dissatisfied with the
agency's record. In 1976 he complained that NEH was "95 percent
academically oriented," adding that "we cannot justify the expend-

iture of taxpayers' money in support of the humanities if the tendency of the program is to proliferate volumes of humanistic studies in university libraries just for other academic humanists to read." He urged NEH to "shift its orientation away from academe and toward greater public responsibility."[10]

Nowhere was his conviction more apparent than in a 1975 Senate speech in which he supported the confirmation of Duffey as NEH chairman. "I care intensely about the welfare of this program," Pell declared. "I have followed it with close attention through these many years, and have seen certain weaknesses and shortcomings in it in the past." His concern was deep, he said, because the humanities "serve to translate knowledge into wisdom. We need that wisdom— and, above all, we need it to be broadly available to us as a nation." Pell called upon the new chairman to "establish new relationships with state governments and new ways to disseminate the values of the humanities at state and local levels," and concluded by expressing his confidence that the new chairman "has that sense of mission required to reinvigorate the humanities, and to give them a new sense of direction and purpose for the betterment of our nation as a whole."[11]

In the course of this speech Pell never mentioned the name of Ronald Berman, but it was clear that when he spoke of NEH's "weaknesses and shortcomings" he was referring to the Berman incumbency. Opposing Berman's renomination, Pell labeled him an elitist who had not done enough to support public programs in the humanities, an opinion that was soon to resurface in remarks to the *New York Times:* "The Humanities Endowment has not realized its full potential to provide opportunities for the enrichment of American life. To do so it must enlist broader participation in quality programs."[12] NEH, Pell argued, was but a "pale shadow" of NEA; the arts had done "a far better job than the humanities in developing diversified, popularly supported, constructive programs at a grassroots level."[13]

In criticizing NEH, Pell frequently brought up the notion of visibility. Because the agency lacked visibility, he argued, the general public was largely unaware of its existence. But if the state humanities committees were to become part of the "warp and woof" of state government, as the state arts councils already were, this would increase the agency's visibility. Berman opposed this plan.

Calling the present arrangement an apparent success, he argued that making the programs wards of the state would render them less flexible. Moreover, projects at the grass-roots level would be less likely to receive funding. Berman also worried that if Pell's plan was enacted the state humanities committees would become politicized, with grants going to groups that state governors wished to appease. Although Berman was a Republican, many felt it was not so much his general political views as his stand on the state humanities committees that had prompted Pell to oppose his renomination.

Pell succeeded in preventing Berman's reappointment, but he was not altogether successful in winning Congress over to his plan for an augmented role for the state committees. The reauthorizing legislation passed in 1976 and 1980 contained some of Pell's recommendations but by no means all of them, for the simple reason that most of the state committees opposed the plan and lobbied strongly against it.

This controversy is tinged with a peculiar irony. In 1977 Pell enthusiastically supported Duffey's confirmation, presumably because he believed Duffey would agree with his plan. Yet two years later Duffey, like Berman, felt compelled to oppose it. He too remained unpersuaded that making the state committees part of the "warp and woof" of state government was the most effective way to encourage support for the humanities at the grass-roots level. But even though he did not get his way completely, Pell dominated the debate about the purpose of NEH. It was Pell who held NEA up as a model for NEH to emulate; it was Pell who questioned NEH's close connection with the scholarly community; and it was Pell who insisted that NEH spend more of its funds on public programs.

Senator Pell should not be singled out as the only member of Congress interested in shaping the development of NEH. Certainly the agency in the first fifteen years of its existence has often appeared to address his concerns, but other congressmen have shown an interest in NEH. By and large, their criticisms and suggestions have resembled Pell's. For instance, Representative Sidney Yates of Illinois, who chairs the House subcommittee responsible for the agency's appropriations, pointedly asked Duffey in 1979: "Do you consciously or unconsciously accord special status to the people of academia, and do you thereby give short shrift to those who do not hold prominent roles in the humanities constituency?"[14] It is doubtful that many congressmen believe that the agency's mission has actually been thwarted by scholars in the humanities, but some have suggested that NEH routinely gives too much support to a small number of scholars clustered at the nation's leading universities.

A look at Duffey's relationship with Congress reveals just how far apart NEH and Congress have been in their understanding of the nature of the agency's mandate. Even though Duffey was the appointee of an administration that believed "the main purpose of the humanities endowment is to touch the lives of ordinary citizens,"[15] his relations with Congress were strained. In 1979 a House report accused NEH of favoring the academic establishment and relying too heavily on a "closed circle" of reviewers,[16] and in 1980 Representative Yates engaged Duffey in a lengthy debate over the extent to which NEH was meeting the needs of the "underserved."[17]

Yates began by questioning the fairness of NEH's review procedures. Citing a letter from a Virginia community college that believed its application to have been rejected because of "elitist attitudes" on the part of the proposal's reviewers,[18] Yates expressed concern that the agency had become the preserve of a narrow academic elite. He also wondered whether institutions truly in need of support in the humanities were losing out in the review process because of their ineptitude in grant preparation. Implying that grantsmanship distorts the competitive process, Yates borrowed a point from the House report, which had made much of the "little guys who are honestly trying to implement excellent ideas but are unable to express it in the same fashion as the professional grantsman."[19] Yates urged NEH to avoid slighting the "little guys" by "set[ting] up an office so that people can come there and you will help them fill out their applications."[20]

Duffey tried to meet Yates halfway. He pointed out that the agency had been trying "to reach some of these constituencies that do not compete with the same advantage as others, and that do require and deserve an extra amount of attention."[21] In fact, the agency was asking for funds to expand its efforts in this area—funds for more staff visits and workshops in the "underserved areas" of the country. But he also reminded Yates that a grantee is not necessarily the ultimate beneficiary of a particular project—that a grant to Harvard, for instance, might indirectly benefit other institutions that needed to strengthen their courses in the humanities. Moreover, Duffey resisted the notion that NEH was unfair or elitist simply because more of its funds went to major universities than to the "little guys." "We have a mandate," he declared "to support the study and nurture of the humanities. . . . In fulfilling this mandate, the Endowment, as a federal agency, can offer, it can administer, it can even on occasion persuade, but it cannot do."[22]

Duffey's point was that NEH is primarily concerned with the support of the humanities, not with the distribution of subsidies to the needy: "We cannot distribute equal ability to compete; there are limits to what we can do. . . . We can't write applications for people."[23] The agency could shape the distribution of grants only by abandoning the procedure of peer review, something it was not prepared to do. When Yates returned to the question of grantsmanship, remarking that the review process should be so simple that a person would not get a rejection merely because he was not prepared, Duffey interrupted him: "I don't think we ought to make it that simple. I don't think I share that objective. We ought not to make it too easy to get a grant. Otherwise, we have an entitlement program. There should be some achievement here."[24]

Although Congress has never suggested that NEH set up an entitlement program, it has often expressed interest in the distribution of grants. In 1973 it authorized the chairman of NEH to "insure that the benefit of its programs will also be available to citizens where such programs would otherwise be unavailable due to geographic or economic reasons." Senators and congressmen frequently ask NEH about the percentage of grants going to their states or congressional districts. NEA and NSF have also been subject to these questions, with NSF somewhat more outspoken than either NEA or NEH in its resistance to congressional appeals for a better distribution of grants. When he was chairman of NSF, Leland Haworth maintained that "to achieve high quality results requires going where the best capability exists. That capability is now quite concentrated geographically."[25] Perhaps because Congress assumes that research in the sciences is critical to the nation, whereas research in the humanities is not, it tends to be less concerned about the unequal distribution of grants to scientists. To put it another way, Congress usually accedes to NSF's argument that it is in the national interest to support the work only of the best scientists, regardless of where they work, but puts up more resistance to similar arguments advanced by NEH.

This is not to say that congressmen by and large regard NEH simply as a pork barrel. Rather, they argue—or at least imply—that NEH was created to meet the need for Americans to understand and appreciate the humanities more fully, and they assume that this need will be met by awarding grants to the needy rather than to Harvard or Stanford or Yale. Like his predecessors, Duffey argued that the distribution of grants is not an accurate measure of NEH's efforts to improve teaching in or to increase public understanding of the humanities, since major universities not infrequently run projects—for example, to revise the curriculum in a particular discipline—that improve the teaching of the humanities at one of the "little guys."[26]

The story of NEH's development, then, has been an ongoing tale of congressional concerns and NEH's attempts to address them. During the Keeney and Berman incumbencies the agency tried to find ways of expending a greater proportion of its funds on public programs. Later, with Duffey at the helm, it sought to effect a more equitable distribution of grants in all categories of support. Yet despite the agency's efforts Congress continued to accuse NEH of not trying hard enough to ensure that those who truly needed support in the humanities were getting it.

No doubt Congress has affected the development of NEH to a great degree, but so too have its chairmen, especially Duffey, who tried to mold the agency into conformity with his views of the humanities in general and of NEH's mandate in particular. When Duffey assumed the chairmanship, he was of course eager to win friends on Capitol Hill for the agency, but he was also animated by the notion that NEH had been the preserve of scholars who had limited ideas of culture. He most emphatically did not "favor a federal agency which establishes at the center norms and values, canons of taste, and accepted definitions of worth to be propagated to the provinces."[27]

As if to stress his view of the humanities, Duffey invited Robert Coles, a Harvard psychiatrist who had often written about Americans who were not well versed in "high culture," to speak at his installation ceremony. In his speech, Coles maintained that the humanities go even further than (as Matthew Arnold would have it) "the best that has been thought and said." The humanities, he claimed, include other voices as well:

> . . . blues and jazz, gospel songs and working songs, . . . the sayings and memories and rituals of countless millions of working people; the blunt, earthy self-justifications and avowals of desperate but determined migrant workers; the wry, detached stories handed down on Indian reservations, in Eskimo villages, generation after generation, . . . the cries of struggle and hope of Appalachians . . . put into traditional ballads and bluegrass music. . . . [Those involved in the humanistic disciplines] should strive to do justice to the richness and diversity of cultural life in a nation whose people are not, many of them, afraid to say what is on their minds.[28]

Duffey, clearly in agreement with Coles's all-encompassing view of the humanities, believed that Americans "in this pluralistic age [are unlikely] to argue that the study of the humanities should be so tightly bound to a single philosophy like the one [Irving] Babbitt called humanism."[29] Later he added, "We are today confronted by the reality of pluralism: the pluralism of participants and contributors to the work of the humanities, the pluralism of subjects of investigation and resources, the pluralism of various cultural heritages within our society."[30] For Duffey, formal recognition of the cultural diversity of Americans was the order of the day.

Some observers regarded this new view of the humanities as a cynical political ploy. According to Hilton Kramer, for instance, the "grass-roots concept of culture" enunciated by Duffey was "likely to be little more than the old political pork barrel dressed up to look like a quaint horn of plenty."[31] But Duffey had not taken up the cause of cultural pluralism simply to ensure a broader distribution of grants. While no doubt aware of the political payoff that the notion of cultural pluralism would yield, he was at the same time strongly influenced by the academy. Many scholars had come to embrace the new view of the humanities, and by the mid-1970s social history had become an important subdiscipline of history. Folklore, too, had become recognized as a distinct subdiscipline. Duffey's view of the humanities was thus welcomed in many quarters. Testifying before Congress in 1980, William Ferris, the director of the Center for Southern Folklore in Memphis, Tennessee, spoke for many scholars when he declared that "the lives of ordinary American people have assumed a place beside volumes of European classics in the humanities." Scholars in the humanities, he insisted, "must recognize those voices which seldom touch the printed page."[32]

Ferris's point was not that NEH should distribute grants more widely but rather that scholars in the humanities should widen their horizons. In theory, cultural pluralism was an attractive notion, a palliative to the high-toned, narrow humanism of an Irving Babbitt. Yet in practice the flag of cultural pluralism was interpreted as a signal that under Duffey's chairmanship NEH not only would broaden the scope of the humanities but would also strive to find ways of achieving a more representative distribution of grants. The *Thirteenth Annual Report,* written under Duffey's chairmanship, suggested a new yardstick to be used in judging the effectiveness of NEH's programs: "Did the Endowment reach as many as possible of the diverse groups in American society that contribute in their own way to the country's culture?"[33] Duffey himself frequently mentioned NEH's new responsiveness to groups that had not been generously funded in the past.

Being responsive meant several things. It meant instituting more representative review panels; Duffey admitted that in some areas NEH had "established goals for representation."[34] Being responsive meant that the staff of NEH would devote more time to encouraging members of certain targeted groups to apply for grants. Being responsive meant publishing a brochure urging Hispanics to seek information about NEH programs by writing or calling NEH's "Hispanic Program Coordinator."[35] Yet responsiveness could backfire by raising expectations that could not be fulfilled. Duffey was powerless to guarantee that the amount of money awarded to Hispanics would increase if more Hispanics applied for grants.

NEH was thus obliged to make applications from members of targeted minority groups more competitive in the review process, and the agency's 1980 budget included funds with which to provide "experts and other kinds of assistance to groups of persons who, by virtue of education, geography, economic conditions, have been underserved in the humanities."[36] But what exactly did "underserved" mean? Apparently it meant that the proportion of grants that a minority group was winning from NEH was unequal to its representation within the general population.

When Duffey began to translate the notion of cultural pluralism into the need to serve the underserved, he made life more difficult for NEH. The concept of the underserved is a Pandora's box from which innumerable groups—ethnic or otherwise—may emerge to claim their "fair" share of grants. In 1980, for example, Representative Mario Biaggi of New York contended that "Americans of Eastern and Southern European origin have been drastically underrepresented as . . . recipients of [NEA and NEH] funds." Biaggi pointed out, as Coles had done three years earlier, that "we are a pluralistic nation and we must be persistent in assuring that we remain so in the artistic and cultural fields."[37] The god of cultural pluralism, Biaggi implied, could be assuaged only by a rigorously representative distribution of grants.

By endeavoring to persuade Congress that NEH under his chairmanship would be more responsive to the underserved, Duffey may have made the problem of distribution somewhat more acute than it might otherwise have been. It would have been a problem, however, even if Duffey had not preached the virtues of cultural pluralism, for the fact was that Duffey, in attempting to shape NEH according to his understanding of its mandate, had left himself little room in which to maneuver. He was constrained by his close ties to the Carter administration.

The Johnson, Nixon, and Ford administrations had never been greatly concerned with NEH. In 1964 President Johnson had expressed a vague interest in a national humanities foundation, but the actual creation of NEH and NEA was mainly the work of Congress, not the executive branch. Nixon, too, had expressed his support for NEH, sending a special message to Congress in 1969 in which he requested that the budgets of the endowments be doubled, but Nixon himself paid virtually no attention to the work of NEH; the message had been drafted by a special assistant, Leonard Garment. Nor did Ford appear to consider NEH a high-priority matter. By contrast, Carter at first appeared to take an intense interest in the future of NEH, announcing that he "want[ed] to be sure that any elitist attitude is ended" within the Endowment.[38] Soon Carter became involved in the search for a new chairman, reportedly grumbling that he was spending more time on that project than he was on the MX missile.[39] Once Duffey was found and confirmed as chairman, the Carter administration was at pains to clarify what it thought NEH's broad policy should be. At the ceremony at which Duffey was installed as chairman, Vice-President Mondale expressed the administration's view that NEH "must lead the search for new ways to share the lessons of our scholarship ever more widely."[40] And his wife, Joan, who became honorary chairman of the Federal Council on the Arts and the Humanities, spoke out in 1978 for rejection of the "imperious aristocracies of academia."[41]

But after Duffey had assumed office, the Carter administration's interest in NEH appeared to wane rapidly. The administration certainly hoped that Duffey would be responsive to blacks and Hispanics, two groups that had been instrumental in Carter's election, but the agency was not important enough to remain a continuing concern, and the articulation of NEH policy was left largely to the new chairman, in a manner reminiscent of earlier administrations. In any event, even if the White House wanted to keep a close watch on the agency, it could not do much to change the policies of the chairman of NEH, who is appointed to a four-year term of office and does not serve at the pleasure of the president.

If the White House is influential in shaping the development of NEH only in that it chooses the chairman, what about the role of the academic community? Since the *1964 Report* was the product of a commission set up by three scholarly organizations, academe was largely responsible for the creation of NEH. But the scholarly community did not get exactly what it expected. As Robert Lumiansky, the president of the American Council of Learned Societies, summed it up in 1979: "We called for a 'National Humanities Foundation' parallel to the National Science Foundation, but we settled for what we got."[42] "Settled" implies that ACLS recognized that NEH was obliged to spend more than NSF did on public programs, but it was surely disappointed at the huge slice of NEH's budget—approximately 50 percent—that went for the support of public programs.

The influence of the academy on NEH has been limited, but the agency has nevertheless been closely associated with formal scholarship. It seems reasonably clear that Congress had intended this to be so, since it defined the humanities as a particular set of academic disciplines rather than simply the purview of people who are interested in learning and culture. Humanists are professionals, people known less for their values than for their expertise in particular areas of knowledge, expertise they have largely (although not necessarily) acquired in the course of graduate education. Most have received doctorates in humanistic disciplines. They are also professionals in that most, although not all, earn their living by teaching as well as pursuing research in those disciplines. Even if Congress were to insist that NEH devote most of its funds to public programming, it is difficult to see how the agency could sever its connections with these scholars, since the creation of public programs requires their assistance.

Trying to come up with evidence that Ronald Berman had been less than sufficiently energetic in his support of public programs in the humanities, Senator Pell asked Berman in 1976: "Do you have any idea of . . . the rough percentage of funds awarded to people who are natural humanists?"[43] The question was unfair, since "natural humanists"—presumably those interested in the humanities but lacking professional training in any humanistic discipline—are rare birds. Most scholars of the humanities are academicians. The only "public" that consistently testifies in behalf of NEH is composed of scholars and the officers of scholarly associations. There are, no doubt, some "natural" humanists in America—the late Eric Hoffer, for instance, may have been one—but there will never be large numbers of them. With the exception of the members of state humanities committees, there simply is no strong public constituency for NEH.

The academy, in addition to being NEH's largest constituency, is also a major force in grant-making decisions, since it is the leading supplier of reviewers for the peer review process. Neither Senator Pell, despite his concern that NEH is too closely connected with the academic community, nor any other congressman has ever suggested that NEH abandon the procedure of peer review. Congress apparently realizes that the confidence of the scholarly community in NEH's grant-making procedures is essential if NEH is to pursue its mandate successfully.

But the notion of a unified community of scholars in the humanities, given that such scholars are notoriously reluctant to see themselves as part of a distinctive community, is a fiction. It was not until 1978 that the first general membership organization for scholars in the humanities, the American Association for the Advancement of the Humanities, was formed. It never succeeded in attracting more than 2,500 members and was forced to suspend operations in August 1982. More than a year earlier, in March 1981, the National Humanities Alliance had been formed in order to lobby against the Reagan administration's proposed cuts in the budgets of NEH and other agencies supporting humanistic work. The alliance, a loose coalition of four organizations, including ACLS, may be longer-lived.

National organizations that look to NEH for support have had some influence on the agency's development, however. ACLS has obviously played a major role in the history of NEH, not only in the initial lobbying effort to create the agency but also in mustering scholarly support for the agency throughout its history. ACLS, it should be noted, has been a major beneficiary of NEH funds, having been awarded, in addition to several grants to support fellowship programs, a $1 million matching grant in 1981 to raise private funds, and several large grants for particular scholarly projects, among them a *Dictionary of the Middle Ages* and an edition of the works of William James. The Association of Research Libraries has probably played a major role in bringing to the attention of NEH and Congress the plight of research libraries. Finally, the Federation of Public Programs in the Humanities, an association of state humanities committees, has become a powerful lobbying force. Created in 1978 and supported primarily by dues from the fifty state humanities committees, the federation keeps a close watch on the way NEH allocates its funds, lobbying against proposed cuts in the amount of money given to State Programs, the NEH division that supports the state committees. The federation's strong interest in the State Programs budget is understandable: the state humanities committees, unlike other humanistic institutions, are dependent upon NEH for their very existence, although some do receive funds from their states and some have received donations from corporations and foundations.

The federation is actually a lobby created by NEH, since the agency indirectly supplies the funds that enable the federation to exist. It tries to protect not only the funds allocated to State Programs but also the existence of the individual state committees. Although each committee must submit a proposal for peer review every two years, no committee (with one exception early in the history of State Programs) has ever been judged and found wanting by the peer review process; no state humanities committee's funds have ever been cut off because its program was judged to be of poor quality. Thus, while NEH provides funds for the existence of state humanities committees, it does not exercise any real control over their programs.

Perhaps because he thought it would be fruitless to try to improve the programs of state committees, which have been criticized for their support of projects only marginally in the humanities, Duffey paid little attention to them. Bennett, however, has decided to try to improve them; chairman's awards for excellence and threats of funding cuts for poor peer reviews are his carrot and stick. Yet it is unlikely that Bennett, or for that matter any chairman of NEH, would be able to cut off funds from a state humanities committee without causing a political storm.

NEH enjoys what an observer in the *New York Times* referred to as a "multiple constituency" consisting of a "strong and willful Congress that knows what the job should be, the scholarly community, the administration, and all the interlocked bodies of government that deal in the same turf."[44] One of the "interlocked bodies," of course, is NEA, yoked together with NEH under the rubric of the National Foundation for the Arts and the Humanities. To some small degree, NEH and NEA do "deal in the same turf"— both agencies, for example, give grants for museum exhibitions— yet in general they serve different constituencies and have little to do with each other.

Nevertheless, owing to the peculiarities of the authorizing legislation, NEA has had a major, albeit indirect, influence on the development of NEH, and particularly on its budget. When the two agencies were founded they were given equal appropriations on the assumption that the needs of the arts and the humanities were roughly equivalent. This notion of parity governed Congress for a number of years. The actual annual appropriations for the two agencies, as opposed to the appropriations set by the legislation reauthorizing the agencies' existence, began to differ in the late 1970s, but it was not until 1980 that the appropriation ceilings set for each agency by the reauthorizing legislation differed. Even then the difference was minimal: the upper limit for appropriations for NEA was set at $1 million more than that for NEH in 1981, and will be $2.5 million more in 1985.

Budget parity benefited NEH more than NEA because NEA, early in its existence, built up an effective lobbying force in its own behalf. There may have been more supporters in Congress for a national humanities foundation than for a national arts foundation in 1965, but by the mid-1970s it was apparent to many congressmen that "support for the arts [was], increasingly, good politics." Leonard Garment, a special assistant to President Nixon, so described support for the arts in a memorandum to the president urging him to ask for increased support for NEA and NEH. "By providing substantially increased support for cultural activities," Garment added, "you will gain support from groups which have hitherto not been favorable to this administration."[45] It was a dubious argument, but Nixon was persuaded.

Garment's influential role as advocate for increased arts and humanities budgets has often been noted. In a 1974 letter to the editor of the *New York Times,* Ronald Berman gave credit for increasing federal support of culture to "the bipartisan wisdom of Congress and the persuasiveness of Leonard Garment," who "translated cultural needs into effective political terms."[46] Berman evidently failed to note that, although Garment did mention the humanities in his memorandum to the president, his argument centered on support for the arts. There were few people in 1974 who thought support for the humanities "good politics."

Leonard Garment was by no means alone in advocating an increased budget for NEA. Nancy Hanks, appointed by Nixon to the chairmanship of NEA in 1969, became so effective an advocate for her agency that an observer in the *Christian Science Monitor* commented in 1977: "It's a good thing that every federal agency doesn't have a Nancy Hanks. Why? Nancy Hanks . . . has a way with Presidents, senators, congressmen; they keep increasing her budget. She also has a way with people across the country. She has helped nurture a growing grass-roots constituency for culture, which keeps calling for those budget increases."[47] Many congressmen were effusive in their praise of Hanks. Representative Jim Wright of Texas, for example, claimed in 1974 that, largely as the result of her effort and ability, NEA "appears to have come as close as any other federal program to achieving excellence."[48] NEH received far fewer plaudits from congressmen, and Berman was not nearly so popular with Congress as Hanks, yet NEH basked in the reflected success of NEA. Had NEH not been yoked to NEA, its budget would have increased much less dramatically in the early 1970s. Because of the linkage, when NEA's budget increased, so did NEH's.

NEH was affected by its association with NEA in other ways as well. It suffered when NEA was held up as a model of what NEH could become, a comparison that was at least partly responsible for the increasing percentage of NEH's budget allocated to public programming. But it benefited when its relationship with NEA obscured debate about its own problems; it was difficult for Congress and the press to focus distinctly on the issue of federal support for the humanities, pro or con. Recently, for example, the lead story in the *Washington Post*'s "Show" section was entitled "Cutting the Endowments"—a misleading headline, for the debate focused only on NEA. Indeed, articles about the two agencies more often than not focus on NEA, thus blurring the distinction between the two agencies in the minds of both the public and Congress.

Even if public and congressional debate had all along focused specifically on NEH, questions about the agency would still remain, for its enabling legislation is far from clear on a number of matters. It calls, for example, for the "pursuit of a national policy for the promotion of progress and scholarship in the humanities" without making evident just what sort of policy is envisioned. Thus, Robert Brustein felt justified in criticizing NEH for failing "to define a national policy on the humanities."[49] Yet it can be argued, as Duffey has pointed out, that if Congress had wanted a national policy for the humanities it would have legislated a Department of the Humanities rather than an endowment which, operating as a government foundation, is concerned only with a policy of support for the humanities.[50]

In short, the legislation does not make clear whether NEH should devote most of its efforts to the support of scholarship or to increasing public appreciation of the humanities. Congress has traditionally regarded the latter as the agency's primary mandate, but other supporters of NEH disagree. In 1980, for example, a Heritage Foundation report criticized the agency for compromising its original aims by supporting projects only peripheral to the humanities, especially projects designed for the general public and centering on questions of public policy, apparently failing to realize that NEH had begun to support such projects in response to Congress's concern about its lack of visibility. NEH insisted that the state committees focus on public policy in the belief that this would be the bait, so to speak, that would awaken public interest in programs in the humanities.

Another difficulty that has plagued NEH has been the constant need to explain what is meant by the humanities, a request that has been put to the chairman of NEH at virtually every congressional hearing. Former Representative Albert H. Quie, for instance, at a meeting of state committees, asked: "What is a *definition* of the humanities which most people can understand? . . . I would welcome any of you who would be willing to send me a one-page letter attempting to *describe* the humanities. . . . You do not face in Congress a negative mood toward the humanities nor do you compete with any lobby who feels we should terminate our programs of federal support. Rather, you face a situation where leaders in government do not for the most part understand or appreciate the humanities."[51]

If Congress itself is unsure of what is meant by the term, it is hard to see how NEH can win the public over to an appreciation of the humanities, or even, for that matter, to remembering the term itself. A reporter who covers the "intellectual beat" for the *New York Times* alluded to this difficulty when he remarked, "We don't use the word 'humanities' around here very much, though we're really saying the same thing in a different way, I suppose."[52] It is clear that "humanities" will never become a household word, but the obscurity of the term has not so much affected the development of the agency as it has engendered tedious gropings toward a definition. In any case, scholars in the different disciplines subsumed under the rubric of the humanities rarely agonize over whether a particular proposal is deficient in that mysterious ingredient called humanistic content.

A more important factor in the ongoing debate about NEH has been the inflated claims made on behalf of the humanities, first in the *1964 Report* and subsequently by certain defenders of NEH. By raising expectations that the values instilled by the humanities, if they were better appreciated by the general public, would improve the quality of American life, these defenders made it inevitable that

Congress would demand more public programming. And by harping on the idea that the humanities embody values at all, they may have made it easier for some fundamentalist Christians to see humanism—an "ism" somehow derived from a study of the humanities—as a secular threat to their own values. Although the opponents of so-called secular humanism have mounted only sporadic attacks on NEH, in the future they may increase their outcry, especially against state humanities committees.

In 1981 some observers wondered whether the specter of secular humanism might be invoked by the Reagan administration in support of an argument that NEH should be abolished altogether. It is true that some Reagan supporters vowed their opposition to secular humanism and that others believed the work of both NEH and NEA to lie beyond the scope of government, but the Reagan administration, it turned out, had no plans for doing away with either agency. Perhaps in order to dodge the question, the new administration appointed a task force to take a close look at NEH and NEA. In September 1981 the task force broadly endorsed the work of both agencies. The administration did try to cut both endowments' budgets by 50 percent, but Congress refused to cooperate and the reductions in their appropriations were relatively minor. Indeed, either persuaded by the arguments of NEH supporters or simply reluctant to do battle with a Congress opposed to deep cuts in NEH's budget, the Reagan administration continually increased its budget requests for NEH, from $77 million in 1981 to $96 million in 1982 and $112 million in 1983.

Some observers were also worried that the Reagan administration might appoint a new NEH chairman who was known less for his support of the humanities than for his allegiance to conservative causes. But after a long search, which included a good deal of infighting among various conservative factions about who would be the most appropriate person for the job, the administration nominated William Bennett as chairman. Although a registered Democrat, Bennett had supported Reagan for president and was a self-styled neoconservative who had expressed his views in such journals as *The Public Interest* and *Commentary*. According to *Time*, Bennett "aroused the suspicion of the arts and humanities constituencies . . . that the NEH will begin to reflect the partisan conservative attitudes of his political sponsors."[53] In most quarters, however, any suspicion was tempered with relief that the administration had appointed someone with a strong background in the humanities, and someone, moreover, who was not closely associated with the Reagan administration.

The appointment of Bennett prompted some conservatives to rejoice that NEH would now veer dramatically from the course it had followed under Duffey. Yet the ardent hopes of some, like the dire fears of others, were excessive, for the difference between Bennett and Duffey, like the difference between Duffey and Berman, was less than had been imagined. Bennett, for example, announced that he would cut the budget for public programs, especially for grants for media projects, but Duffey had already begun to make the same cuts before he left office. Although Bennett stressed the importance of improving the teaching of the humanities where Duffey had not, both chairmen believed that support for the academy should take precedence over public programs.

There were several reasons for this shift in emphasis. For one thing, some public programs were prohibitively expensive: ventures in the media, for example, were extremely costly, and few proved to be of lasting value. Second, some public programs, especially those produced by unions and national organizations, fell only marginally within the scope of the humanities, and some were controversial, a point that is discussed in chapter 8. Third, there was general disillusionment with the effectiveness of public programs, especially since only a few grants—to museums for "blockbuster" exhibits—generated large audiences.

NEH, moreover, was coming increasingly to realize that the humanities were faring poorly within academe. Research funds were drying up as private foundations reduced their support of scholarship in the humanities. More significantly, major research libraries were increasingly burdened with mounting costs not only because of the new profusion of materials but also because of rapidly deteriorating holdings. Finally, undergraduate education in the humanities was weak in a number of areas, and it was unlikely that a large public audience for programs in the humanities would emerge from a college-educated population whose education in these areas had been poor. If the humanities did not flourish in the academy it was unlikely that they would ever flourish elsewhere. NEH needed to husband its limited resources and concentrate on those areas that actually sustained the humanities.

This change in emphasis began during the final two years of Duffey's term of office and continued into Bennett's chairmanship. Unfortunately, at the same time, the debate about NEH became obscured by the terms "populist" and "elitist," with Berman viewed as elitist in contrast to the populist Duffey. Duffey was indeed a populist insofar as his notion of the humanities included social history and folklore, but in that sense many scholars in the humanities are populists. If populism implies a preoccupation with the development of more public programs in the humanities, then Berman was more of a populist than Duffey. If it means dedication to the task of awarding grants to members of minority groups, then Duffey was a populist and Berman was not. And even Duffey was less zealous than Congress on the broad question of the equitable distribution of grants.

Elitist and populist, then, are not particularly useful terms with which to describe the major participants in the debate over NEH's mandate in the 1970s. Nor are Democratic and Republican labels any more helpful. It was the Republican Berman, after all, who vastly expanded NEH's efforts in the area of public programs, and the Democratic Duffey who began to cut back on public programs. Yet partisan politics did play a part in the history of NEH, for, with the exception of Keeney, the agency's chairmen were chosen as much for their political affiliations as for their distinction as scholars in the humanities.

Despite a series of political appointments, the debate about NEH policy did not take a strongly partisan turn until the appointment of Duffey. Some observers were alarmed not so much by Duffey himself as by the Carter administration's expressed interest in changing NEH policy. Implying that under its Republican chairman NEH had been sufficiently devoted neither to cultural pluralism nor to a truly representative distribution of grants, the Carter administration plainly wanted to see a significant increase in grants to blacks, Hispanics, and women. Carter succeeded in changing the emphasis of the debate about NEH policy. The main question was no longer whether NEH should allocate most of its funds to the academy or to public programs. Rather, it was whether NEH should devote itself to honoring excellence in the humanities or to making a strong effort to seek out and help the humanistically impoverished. In order to show that he was trying to help blacks, Hispanics, and women to get more grants, Duffey created new staff positions—liaisons to minority groups. These staff members would help minority applicants with their proposals, if not exactly write them. Duffey also tried to ensure that more members of minority groups were chosen to serve as peer reviewers.

Bennett, who had coauthored (with Terry Eastland) a book critical of the notion of affirmative action (*Counting by Race: Equality from the Founding Fathers to Bakke and Weber*), abolished the liaison positions and declared that NEH would no longer hold workshops intended only for members of minority groups. There was little outcry over these actions, perhaps because changes in the staffing of NEH are not usually reported by the press. One year after Bennett had taken office, the controversy about public programs vis-à-vis support for the academy had largely subsided. So had the debate over whether or not NEH should make an effort to ensure a representative distribution of grants. What remained as a subject of debate was the scope of the humanities, with Bennett implying that his view was closer to that of Irving Babbitt than it was, say, to that of Robert Coles. In remarks such as "I don't think you can have a liberal arts college without a classics department,"[54] Bennett was not actually opposing social history or folklore; he was instead stressing his view of the humanities as consisting of a relatively limited and traditional core of materials.

In sum, the politics of NEH do not make for a particularly edifying story. It has been a tale of misunderstandings about NEH's mandate, confusion over the nature of the humanities, foolish expectations of "visibility," and an often misguided zeal to achieve a wide and representative distribution of grants. It is only by looking behind this story that we can discern in rough outline the makings of an important debate about the scope of the humanities and the broad purpose of NEH's existence.

4

The Peer Review Process

DESPITE major differences between the National Endowment for the Humanities and the other two federal grant-making agencies with which it has often been compared, the three agencies are similar in one important respect: NEH, NEA, and NSF all rely upon the peer review procedure when making decisions about awards. For NEH, this procedure is intrinsic to a process by which, in 1981, 2,632 grants were awarded to 7,882 applicants. The procedure involves the participation of thousands of private citizens (in 1981 they numbered 5,376) who review individual proposals, which they receive by mail, or serve as members of review panels that meet in Washington to assess a batch of proposals.[1] Most proposals submitted to the Research Division, for example, are evaluated by five to eight outside reviewers who are specialists in their fields and who assess each proposal "within the framework of [its] particular discipline or field." NEH next convenes panels of scholars from different fields "to weigh [each] proposal in competition with others for the funds allocated to that particular program."[2] Finally, the opinions of both reviewers and panelists are conveyed to the National Council, which meets four times a year, each session lasting two days, to make recommendations to the chairman of NEH, who has sole grant-making authority.

The opinions of scholars in the humanities are obviously the major factor in the peer review process, but the NEH staff does play a supporting role. It chooses both the reviewers and the panelists, and in some cases, especially those in which there is strong disagreement among reviewers or panelists about the merits of a proposal, it is asked by the National Council for its opinion. The National Council also plays a role, but because it has so many applications to consider, this role is generally perfunctory, except in cases in which large sums of money are involved.

These peer review procedures resemble those of both NEA and NSF, but there are some differences. NSF relies more heavily than does NEH on the opinions of outside reviewers. As an NSF brochure puts it, "All proposals are reviewed carefully by a scientist serving as an NSF program officer and usually by three to ten other scientists who are expert in the particular field represented by the proposal."[3] And although NSF sometimes convenes panels to review proposals, it does not always do so, as NEH does. "Peer review," another NSF brochure tells us, "generally takes the form of *ad hoc* mail reviews, reviews by an assembled panel of experts, or a combination of both."[4] Another difference between the two agencies is that NSF's National Board, unlike NEH's National Council, reviews only those proposals requesting more than $500,000. But perhaps the most important difference between the two agencies is that NSF has established advisory committees, appointed for three-year terms, which serve as overseers of particular program areas, at times giving advice on individual proposals but more often simply keeping an eye on their program areas' procedures. Every three years each advisory committee subjects its program area to intensive evaluation. NEA also incorporates advisory committees, appointed for one-year terms renewable for three years, but their members serve as panelists as well as advisers. They both evaluate proposals and "develop the policies and programs through which the Endowment responds to changing conditions."[5] Finally, NEA does not usually make use of outside reviewers.

In sum, we can say that at NEA the opinions of panelists are the central factor in the review process (NEA's National Council, like NEH's, does ostensibly review all applications); at NSF the opinions of outside reviewers are the integral factor; and at NEH both outside reviewers and panelists are central to the review process. But these generalizations tend to obscure some important differences within different program areas. For example, NEH's Fellowship Program does not generally make use of outside reviewers. It relies, rather, on a two-stage panel process. In the first stage, applications are judged by specialists (in effect this first stage takes the place of outside reviews), and in the second, they are evaluated by scholars from different disciplines.

Whatever the differences in their procedures, all three agencies rely heavily on the opinions of independent professionals in making decisions about grants. It is a method that has met with overwhelming approval; no major spokesman for the sciences, arts, or humanities has ever suggested that peer review be abandoned. Nevertheless, over the years there has been a good deal of grumbling that, while in theory peer review is excellent, in practice—at all three agencies and for a variety of reasons—it has been unfair in that it has not always resulted in a representative distribution of grants. Senator Pell implied as much when he asked Ronald Berman whether he had a "feeling for the relationship between the population of each state or each region as opposed to the percentage of funds spent in that region."[6] And Representative Norman Dicks of Washington, after arguing that too many fellowships had gone to scholars at eastern universities, told Joseph Duffey that he hoped "greater attention" would be given to rectifying what he regarded as a geographic imbalance in the distribution of fellowships.[7]

Responding to these complaints, Berman noted vaguely that NEH felt obligated to be "representative," and Duffey assured Congress that he was striving to ensure "equity of support." But precisely what was meant by these phrases is unclear. How, for example, can NEH rectify a geographic imbalance in the distribution of grants when it has no control over either who applies from what state or the quality of the proposals from a particular state? Moreover, is it not likely that certain states will always be awarded a disproportionate share of NEH grants because scholars in the humanities, as well as humanistic institutions such as research libraries and art museums, are not distributed according to the distribution of the population as a whole? There is no doubt that states such as New York and Massachusetts will benefit more from NEH monies than will states such as North or South Dakota, since there are more universities—and therefore more humanistic scholars—in New York and Massachusetts than in North and South Dakota, not only absolutely but also proportionally.

Complaints about unfairness at NEH have not been confined to geographical imbalance. Critics have also alleged that NEH has not made a representative number of grants to blacks, women, and members of minority groups. Yet here, too, it is difficult to see how NEH can ensure representative distribution, since there are proportionately more white scholars than black, more male than female. In 1975–76 whites constituted 81.5 percent of the college-age population and 81 percent of new Ph.D.s in all fields. In the same years 12.4 percent of the college-age population, but only 3.6 percent of those awarded doctorates, were black. (Asian American/Pacific Islanders, in contrast, constituted 0.7 percent of the college-age population, but 1.9 percent of those awarded doctorates.) In 1976 women constituted 51 percent of the college-age population, but only 23.3 percent of those awarded doctorates. More significantly, in 1979 (the first year for which these statistics are available), out of 4,143 doctorates awarded in the humanities, only 130 (approximately 3 percent) went to blacks. Since most professional scholars in the humanities have doctorates, a correlation between the distribution of grants to black scholars and the distribution of blacks in the population as a whole may be a sign not of "equity of support" but of discrimination in their favor.

The problem is complicated by the fact that statistics on the distribution of scholars in the humanities can be misleading. We must break these figures down to reflect the distribution of scholars according to particular disciplines. In most disciplines scholars are disproportionately male, but in some there is a disproportionate number of females. In 1972, 42 doctorates were awarded to men and 40 to women in art history and criticism; in 1979, 65 were awarded to men and 101 to women. By contrast, philosophy has remained disproportionately male; in 1972, 307 doctorates in philosophy were awarded to men and only 41 to women, and in 1979 men received 225, women 52. The annual summary report of scholars receiving doctorates from American universities reveals other, equally significant differences among disciplines.[8]

It is obvious that those concerned with the equitable distribution of grants should pay careful attention to the distribution of the population within particular disciplines, yet it would be an administrative nightmare if NEH were obliged to spend time (and money) correlating, for example, the percentage of philosophers who are female with the percentage of grants going to female philosophers. In any case, even if NEH were to discover that females constituted 10 percent of the philosophy profession yet received only 3 percent of the grants in philosophy, what would be the significance of this statistical discovery? It might reflect only the fact that fewer female than male philosophers had applied for grants.

For some observers, evidence that the distribution of scholars in the humanities is out of balance with the distribution of the general population is a sign that NEH is not doing its job. The agency, they argue, should be concerned with changing the landscape of the humanities—with finding ways, for example, of encouraging more blacks to become scholars. The authorizing legislation makes it clear that NEH is charged with rendering the humanities more central to American life rather than changing the composition of the academy. And even if such a goal had been intended, it is highly unlikely that NEH could do much to meet it. Choosing a profession is a highly individual matter depending upon factors well beyond the control of government, and government can do little to lure people into particular professions. It can, of course, designate certain professions as being in the national interest and can attract people into them with the promise of certain benefits—free tuition, for example—but it cannot persuade, say, more Hispanics to become aeronautical engineers.

We must not make too much of the problem of under- or over-representation. For one thing, although both Duffey and Berman spoke in vague terms about NEH's obligation to be representative, no chairman of NEH has ever promised Congress that the agency would make a strong effort to ensure a representative distribution of grants. Neither has Congress itself, with the exception of Senator Pell, dwelled on the matter. And Pell made much of NEH's lack of representativeness only in the course of his vigorous opposition to Berman's reappointment. Thus, not even Pell has persuasively or consistently called for the representative distribution of grants, presumably because he is well aware that such representativeness would transform NEH from an agency that awards grants into one that bestows entitlements according to some complex proportional formula. Finally, NEH does not collect data on race, sex, or ethnic heritage of applicants for awards, although it does, of course, know the geographical location of applicants. Under Duffey's chairmanship NEH did ask those awarded grants to fill out anonymous tearsheets with data on race and ethnic background.

While all past NEH chairmen have been supportive of peer review, Duffey tried to deflect congressional criticism about the distribution of grants by claiming that during his chairmanship NEH would give "priority consideration to the composition of its review panels and [would seek] to secure as broad a representation as possible."[9] In attempting to achieve equitable representation, Duffey set forth goals for the composition of panels, so that representative numbers of blacks, women, American Indians, Hispanics, and Asian Americans would serve on them. In a report to Congress in 1980, he claimed that "the effort to broaden representation on panels by women and minorities has been successful. Next year, no panel will have less than one-third women, and most panels will have 50 percent."[10]

In a public letter to Duffey, Sidney Hook, a former member of the National Council of NEH, objected strenuously to this setting of numerical goals in the selection of panel reviewers. Duffey responded that NEH makes its initial selection of panelists "on the basis of qualification and appropriateness for service,"[11] but failed to explain just how NEH could claim that its main concern was "qualification and appropriateness for service" and at the same time insist that no panel would contain fewer than one-third women. The directives Duffey sent to NEH staffers concerning increasing the proportion of blacks, Hispanics, women, American Indians, and Asian Americans on panels may have had the effect of making the staff, which chooses panelists from a computerized list of more than 20,000 names, more concerned with a would-be panelist's race, sex, or ethnic background than with his qualifications.

If instituting numerical goals for panel reviewers does not actually make it likely that poorly qualified persons will be chosen to serve as reviewers, such an effort to be representative certainly raises expectations that cannot be easily fulfilled. There is no evidence to suggest that a representative panel of reviewers is more likely to recommend a representative distribution of grants. A panel reviewer would not necessarily favor proposals from members of his own sex, race, or ethnic group; indeed, most scholars in the humanities would find such an assumption insulting to their status as professionals. Some may even lean in the opposite direction in order to avoid the slightest taint of unprofessionalism.

The flag of representation has also from time to time been a signal to other groups to complain about being underrepresented on review panels. The American Association of State Colleges and Universities (AASCU), for example, protested in 1977 that only 11 percent of the members of NEH review panels represented AASCU institutions.[12] But even if review panels were composed of a disproportionately large number of scholars from AASCU institutions, there would be no guarantee that a greater number of scholars from those institutions would be awarded grants. Just as black scholars do not automatically recommend proposals from black applicants, so scholars who teach at state universities do not necessarily recommend proposals from their own or other state universities. Surely most panelists when considering proposals are concerned with the intrinsic merit of each proposal rather than with such (to them) extraneous questions as the race or institutional affiliation of the applicant. The primary allegiance of a scholar is to his discipline, not to his race, sex, or institution.

AASCU's complaint about underrepresentation was similar to one expressed in a House report accusing NEH of employing a "closed circle" of reviewers. In response to this report, NEH reaffirmed its intention of ensuring that "all Endowment panels include qualified women, persons from varied ethnic and minority backgrounds, and representatives from a wide range of humanities institutions."[13] In many cases, however, these several goals conflict with one another. If, for example, a disproportionately small percentage of blacks teaches at AASCU institutions, then it may prove very difficult for NEH to increase both the percentage of blacks and the percentage of scholars from AASCU institutions who serve on review panels.

The attempt to have a representative proportion of panel reviewers is further complicated by discord within disciplines. At a recent meeting of the American Philosophical Association (APA), for example, a group of philosophers revolted against the alleged domination of APA by the analytic school of philosophy. Forming their own group, the dissidents argued that the domination of APA by a subgroup had had unfortunate practical consequences: since foundations often turn to APA for the names of reviewers, applicants who are members of the analytic school are favored by the analytic philosophers who serve as reviewers.[14] The nonanalytic philosophers went so far as to complain that their work is not even considered by analytic philosophers to be within the discipline of philosophy. This kind of argument means that NEH, when selecting reviewers to serve on certain panels, sometimes faces the difficult question of deciding who is or is not a qualified scholar in a given field. Philosophy may be the most openly divided of the humanities, but other disciplines are also riddled with factions. Should the NEH staff, then, attempt to ensure that a particular discipline's major factions are represented on panels? It is clear that if the agency tried to meet the objections of all groups claiming to be underrepresented on review panels it would have difficulty convening a single panel.

In addition to complaining about the distribution of grants and an alleged "closed circle" of reviewers, Congress has also accused NEH of "personally grooming" certain applicants, dominating panel procedures, and "with increasing frequency" overriding the judgments of review panels.[15] These charges fail to take into account the fact that the Endowment's various goals require different roles for NEH staff members. The staff should have virtually no say in selecting proposals for scholarly research, since qualified scholars are most capable of judging which applications have merit; in fact, in the Fellowships Division (according to NEH), staff recommendations have differed from those of reviewers only twice in ten years. In considering other kinds of proposals, however, staff opinions may be important, since the knowledge staff members have gained as administrators of grants may give them a better sense than panel reviewers can be expected to have of whether a particular proposal is likely to result in a successful project.

If a significant number of the proposals recommended by peer reviewers were rejected by NEH, the peer review process would be undermined and the scholarly community would lose confidence in NEH, deciding—perhaps rightly so—that the agency had become politicized. Nevertheless, neither the National Council nor the NEH chairman, who has sole grant-making authority, should feel obligated to abide by the judgments of peer reviewers. One reason is that peer reviewers may recommend more proposals than the agency's budget enables it to fund. The chairman, in consultation with the National Council, must ask, as Duffey did: "Should we use public money to pay for this research; is it important enough; is there a national significance to it or a significance to other fields; which ones should we choose at this point if we can fund only 300 out of 2,200?"[16] Then, too, since the chairman alone is answerable to Congress for the operation of NEH, he must reserve the right to view the national interest differently from peer reviewers, the staff, or even the National Council. Naturally, if he were to exercise his authority without prudence and discretion, he would succeed only in jeopardizing his own position.

Some criticisms of NEH's review process have centered neither on the composition of review panels nor on the role of the staff but on the mechanics of the process itself, particularly on its alleged lack of openness. Senator Pell has time and again criticized NEH for not making the names of panelists available before each panel convenes. NEA, which has standing review committees as opposed to reviewers selected only for particular funding cycles, does publish the names of panelists beforehand. It has been Pell's feeling that "the interest of government is in not having meetings of this sort—meetings of people who are not accountable until after their actions."[17] What Pell means by "accountable" is unclear, for how can one be accountable for one's actions before one has acted—in this case, before one has actually reviewed a proposal? Moreover, it is not obvious that revealing the names of reviewers before they have actually served on panels would make the review process more objective. This could in fact have the opposite effect; according to NEH, "experience indicates that when the panelists are identified in advance of the review, some applicants will attempt to contact them and influence them."[18] Most likely, however, the publication of panelists' names beforehand would have little effect on the review process. It might deter a few qualified scholars from serving on panels for fear of being harassed by applicants, but most applicants would probably refrain from lobbying for their own proposals lest they be regarded as unprofessional and therefore hurt their chances for awards.

Some observers have suggested that the procedure of peer review is automatically skewed if applicants provide information about gender and institutional affiliation. During the past decade, there have been complaints that reviewers of scholarly essays submitted for publication in learned journals tend to be better disposed toward articles written by men and/or those written at major research institutions. As a result, many journals have adopted the policy of "blind reviewing," which requires that an author's name, professional rank, and institutional affiliation be removed from his manuscript before it is sent out for review. The difficulty with instituting such a policy at NEH is that review panelists assess proposed work rather than complete work. Reviewers of applications to do scholarly research need information not only about the intrinsic merit of a project but also about the applicant's track record as a scholar. For example, reviewers of applications for Fellowships for Independent Study and Research, the Fellowships Division's only unrestricted category of support, are asked to assess not only the quality of the application but also "the likelihood that the applicant will see the study through to completion." Without any accompanying information, it would be difficult indeed to make this kind of assessment.

In any case, it is unlikely that NEH will adopt a policy of blind reviewing, for the trend is distinctly in the direction of providing more rather than less information about applicants. More information, Congress has assumed, will enable NEH to distribute grants more representatively. The proponents of blind reviewing, of course, disagree; they believe that less information would make for a more representative distribution. For instance, when Helen Vendler, professor of English at Boston University, was president of the Modern Language Association, she argued that women are underrepresented in the pages of *PMLA* (the association's journal) because reviewers of articles are biased against research done by women. As one professor of literature has said, "The policy [of blind reviewing] is a sign that the profession does believe in a meritocracy."[19] Presumably this scholar would continue to support blind reviewing even if the number of articles by women in scholarly journals decreased rather than increased.

The trouble with most schemes to improve the peer review process is that they are based on the assumption that the process is objective only if it results in a representative distribution of grants. Reflecting this assumption, Senator Pell remarked at the Berman renomination hearings: "I understand . . . [that] in fiscal 1975, Ohio State University, with a rather large faculty . . . received in all kinds of grants, not senior fellowship grants but all grants, $134,000, while Yale, a great deal smaller, received $3,300,000." Clearly implying that these figures were evidence that NEH's reviewing procedures were less than objective, Pell asked: "What would be the reason for this disproportion?"[20]

The question is one to which it is virtually impossible to respond. Berman would have had to know how many people from Yale and

Ohio State had applied for grants, for how much money they had applied, and the categories of support under which they had applied. Even then it would have been difficult to decide whether the review procedures had been biased. Suppose that ten scholars from each institution had applied to do research in philosophy, and nine of the Yale applicants but only one from Ohio State were awarded grants. Obvious discrimination? Not necessarily. This distribution of awards would most likely have indicated only that the scholars who served as peer reviewers had considered all twenty applications—considered them, it should be kept in mind, not against one another but as part of a batch of applications from scholars affiliated with many different colleges and universities—and had decided that the chosen ten were more meritorious than the others. During the panel review, it is unlikely that the question of Ohio State vis-à-vis Yale would ever have arisen.

Would the decision have been different if the body of reviewers had been constituted differently, if more reviewers, for instance, had been from institutions like Ohio State than from institutions like Yale? The decision might well have been different, but we cannot say that it would have favored the scholars from Ohio State. One can tinker almost endlessly with the process of peer review, but it will not ensure predictable results. Of course, some reviewers *are* biased, but pursuing the *ignis fatuus* of representation will not eliminate bias. It is the job of the NEH staff to discern which panelists do a poor job of reviewing, for whatever reasons, and to make sure that these reviewers are not reappointed.

When William Bennett became chairman of NEH in 1981, he told the staff that they need not be unduly concerned about achieving representative panels. But even Bennett could not, and did not, abandon the notion of representation, for NEH's authorizing legislation requires that panels "have broad geographic and culturally diverse representation." NEH's *Sixteenth Annual Report,* written under Bennett's chairmanship, was careful to take note of this point in its discussion of peer review.[21]

Few observers believe the notion of representation should be abandoned altogether, but some think that under Duffey the concern with achieving representation became such an overriding one that many poorly qualified scholars were chosen to serve on review panels. Sidney Hook implied as much when he accused NEH under Duffey of having been "transformed into a political tool that amounts to a wholesale subsidization of mediocrity."[22] According to several members of the NEH staff, however, the quest for representative panels had only a minor effect on peer review, with but few panelists chosen more to fulfill a "goal" than for the strength of their professional qualifications. Even if some of the grants made under Duffey's chairmanship were questionable, it would be difficult to prove that an inferior system of peer review was responsible. In any case, the quest for representative panels was not a success, for NEH could find out whether panels were becoming more representative, at least in terms of race and ethnic heritage, only by asking panelists to fill out tearsheets on which each checked off his race and ethnic background—which many scholars refused to do. Some, according to NEH staff members, even wrote angry letters about the unprofessional nature of this request. Thus NEH was never able to accumulate the statistics it had hoped to compile in order to prove to Congress that its panels were more representative than they had been in the past.

There have been complaints not only about the distribution of grants and the composition of review panels but also about the peer review process itself. The National Commission on Research, for example, has criticized the procedure as it is currently employed by most federal agencies supporting research because of the "inability or unwillingness" of reviewers to recognize and recommend support for "highly innovative, high-risk proposals."[23] And science writer Daniel Greenberg has called the peer review process "an inherently bland, responsibility-diluting method that generally tends to caution and conservatism in giving away money." It is doubtful, according to Greenberg, whether "Darwin or Einstein would have got anything more than a curt rejection out of such a system."[24] Finally, a recent study of NSF has revealed that chance plays a significant part in the peer review process. Because there is a good deal of disagreement among scientists about what good science is or should be, "the fate of a particular grant application is roughly half determined by the characteristics of the proposal and the principal investigator, and about half by apparently random elements which might be characterized as the 'luck of the reviewer draw.'"[25]

That the peer review process is both cautious and somewhat arbitrary does not argue for scuttling it altogether. The inherent conservatism of the procedure is entirely appropriate for federal agencies entrusted with public funds. And the element of luck is understandable, given the disagreement that characterizes all scholarly disciplines. NEH's procedures may well be less arbitrary than NSF's, since NEH relies more on review panels in which reviewers can arrive at a consensus about the relative merits of a group of proposals, whereas NSF relies more on evaluations from outside reviewers who have no chance to revise their initial impressions after a discussion with peers. In any case, complaints about the peer review process—both the choice of reviewers and the choice of award-winning proposals—are sure to continue. As Representative Theodore Weiss has observed, "in a situation . . . in which moneys are being granted or disbursed, invariably there are more people who are unhappy than happy."[26]

There has never been a detailed investigation of NEH's peer review procedures, but such an investigation has been made at NSF. In 1977 investigators concluded that "the NSF peer-review system is in general an equitable arrangement that distributes the limited funds available for basic research primarily on the basis of the perceived quality of the applicant's proposal. In particular, we find that NSF does not discriminate systematically against noneminent scientists in the ways that some critics have charged."[27] If a similar investigation were to be made of NEH's peer review procedures, especially its consideration of applications to do research in the humanities, the same conclusions would undoubtedly be reached.

5

Research in the Humanities

IN 1979 Wayne Booth, a professor of English at the University of Chicago, told the National Council that while NEH's grant program was impressive in scope, it left him with "an alarmed sense of threatening miscellaneousness, a feeling that any agency that attempts to do all of these things is doomed to do none of them very well." NEH, he said, must begin by "pruning its portfolio if it is to do its job."[1] Was Booth right? In order to evaluate his criticisms, we must look more closely at what NEH has done in support of research (and, in later chapters, of teaching and public programs) in its attempt to further "national progress in the humanities."

Since the earliest days of the Republic, as we noted in chapter 1, the United States government has encouraged and at times actively supported the advancement of knowledge. The subject was discussed at the Constitutional Convention, with the result that the Constitution empowers Congress "to promote the Progress of Science and useful Arts." Like the other Founding Fathers, George Washington thought the promotion of the arts and the sciences was in the national interest. In his "First Annual Address to Congress" he called for the establishment of a national university, saying that "there is nothing which can better deserve your patronage than the promotion of Science and Literature." In his "Eighth Annual Address to Congress" he repeated his request for a national university, arguing that "a flourishing state of the Arts and Sciences contributes to National prosperity and reputation."[2] He approved, moreover, of the establishment in 1780 of an American Academy of Arts and Sciences that would—so its founders claimed—"cultivate every art and science which may tend to advance the interest, honor, dignity, and happiness of a free, independent, and virtuous people."[3]

It was with some justification, then, that—just as academic scientists had earlier lobbied for a National Science Foundation to support basic research in the sciences—academic humanists expected a national humanities foundation to support basic research in the humanities. They of course realized that some funds would be devoted to the diffusion of humanistic knowledge; the *1964 Report* had, after all, stressed the importance of spreading the gospel of the humanities. But the agency's primary purpose would be the support of humanistic research, and this purpose meant that it would rely heavily on the judgments of professional humanists, most of whom were connected with academia.

But Congress, or rather the handful of congressmen responsible for NEH's reauthorization and appropriations, has all along seen NEH's mission in a different light. Persuaded perhaps by the language of the *1964 Report*, Senator Pell and others have argued that NEH's primary mission is the diffusion of knowledge, and have further insisted that NEH should not be the exclusive preserve of academe. Pell as was noted in chapter 3, often questioned NEH's academic orientation, especially its support for scholarly research. Other congressmen have echoed Pell's remarks—not so much decrying the support of research in the humanities as implying that it is a waste of the taxpayers' money because the research is arcane and trivial.[4]

These contradictory interpretations of NEH's mandate should not be minimized, but they are not irreconcilable. Although Pell has suggested that grants be awarded to those nonprofessionals he terms "natural humanists" as well as to academics, he has never argued that the agency should eliminate all support for the advancement of humanistic knowledge; on the other side of the same coin, professional humanists such as Lumiansky have never suggested that NEH should eliminate all support for the diffusion of knowledge. No doubt Congress and the academy will always disagree about the percentage of NEH's funds that should be allocated to the advancement of humanistic knowledge, but that the agency should provide some support for research is accepted by virtually everyone. After all, its enabling legislation clearly states that NEH should support "progress and scholarship in the humanities." And, as Joseph Duffey has remarked, "Fundamental to all Endowment support activities, and to its goals—whether they involve the public or the academy—is scholarly knowledge."[5]

Nevertheless, Congress's lack of interest in humanistic research as well as its continuing distrust of the academy have hampered NEH's efforts to sponsor original research in the humanities. Only a natural aristocracy, Jefferson would say, is capable of advancing knowledge; only the best professional humanists, judged as such by their peers (whether within the academy or outside of it), can advance humanistic knowledge. Yet in order to avoid congressional criticism, NEH has tried at the very least to muffle its support for the "natural aristocracies" of academia by describing basic humanistic research in terms that make it more palatable to Congress—by describing it, that is, as relevant to contemporary problems. More important, NEH has often tinkered with its programs in support of humanistic research in such a way that merit is neglected, if not actually ignored, and other criteria (for instance, whether or not a project is demonstrably in the national interest) have been emphasized.

At the heart of the problem is the belief of most Americans, even of most professional humanists, that basic research in the hard sciences is of significant benefit to us all, whereas basic research in the humanities is less so. So pervasive is the notion that basic scientific research is the only truly important research that reports published recently by the National Commission on Research pay only scant attention to basic research in the humanities. True, this commission focused on scientific research because the scientific community receives the lion's share—more than 90 percent—of the federal budget for research. Nevertheless, it is notable that when the author of *Review Processes: Assessing the Quality of Research Proposals* describes the benefits that scientific research confers on the nation, he uses the word "research" without modification. "Research," he says, "leads to improvements in agriculture, in the diagnosis and treatment of disease, in technologies which increase productivity and lead to new products; it contributes to the prestige and security of the nation."[6] The point is not so much that basic research in the humanities has been ignored or slighted by the National Commission on Research as that researchers in the humanities can never make the case for federal support as strongly as can researchers in the hard sciences.

The authors of the *1964 Report*, sensing perhaps the difficulty of persuading Congress to authorize an agency devoted to basic research in the humanities, emphasized the need for the diffusion of humanistic concerns, despite the fact that academic humanists expected, as Barnaby Keeney has said, that "the great bulk of [a humanities] endowment's funds would go into support of humanistic research without reference to its utility or relevance."[7] Once the new agency had gotten onto its feet, it evidently became concerned about the possibility that Congress might change its mind about supporting any research at all in the humanities. The *Third Annual Report*, attempting to make research more relevant and hence more palatable, announced that NEH would "give priority in its grant-making to proposals for studies related to contemporary problems."[8] It was not the first nor the last such attempt. In 1968 the National Council expressed its desire "to encourage . . . appropriate project proposals within the various fields of the humanities which are concerned with values as they bear on urbanization, minority problems, war, peace, and foreign policy; problems of Governmental decision, civil liberties and the wider application of humanistic knowledge and insights to the general public interest."[9]

In 1968 and 1970, NEH's original legislation was amended to include, under the term humanities, "the study and application of the humanities to the human environment with particular attention to the relevance of the humanities to the current conditions of national life." And in 1979, after publishing a short pamphlet, *American Social History*, Duffey told Congress that "we have a publication defining that field [in order to] identify an area of clear and definite need in American scholarship."[10]

It is evident that, in its desire to affirm the importance of research in the humanities, NEH emphasized the value of applied research; and Congress, by amending the agency's enabling legislation, signaled its desire for NEH to devote more of its funds to applied research. It is difficult to assess the weight that proposals to do applied research have been given in the grant-making process, but there is no doubt that from time to time NEH has hinted that proposals dealing with certain subjects (especially uniquely American topics) might stand a better chance of being funded than others.

The American Bicentennial provides an example. In the early 1970s NEH's Division of Research allocated approximately 10 per-

cent of its budget for projects relating to the Bicentennial. The agency
had little choice in the matter, for when the American Revolution
Bicentennial Commission was created, Congress mandated that NEH
encourage and coordinate "scholarly works and presentations focusing on the history, culture, and political thought of the Revolutionary War period."[11] In February 1973 the National Council indicated that the Bicentennial should provide a major focus for NEH
programs during the next three years. And the agency itself, in its
information for applicants in its *Eighth Annual Report*, said: "Since
a serious recognition of the Bicentennial will require just the kind
of intelligent nationwide exploration of America that the Endowment was created by Congress to foster, NEH is encouraging the
submission of applications for projects which bring the humanities
to bear on serious study of the American experience from colonial
times to the present, with particular—but not exclusive—emphasis
on the period surrounding the founding of the nation."[12]

The National Council had issued, in its 1968 document, a vague
but extensive shopping list of relevant topics for humanistic research, which prompted the authors of the *Fifth Annual Report* to
remark that "few statements so brief raise such imposing questions
of implementation."[13] If the National Council meant that those concerned with reviewing proposals for humanistic research should give
some extra weight to the relevance of the research being proposed,
it never said so explicitly. And after presenting its varied list of
relevant topics, it stressed that "each proposal, regardless of its emphasis in this respect, will be judged primarily on its instrinsic
merit."[14] The relevance of the subject matter, then, has probably
been only a minor consideration in the awarding of grants to do
research, for peer reviewers have never been asked to consider whether
a particular proposal deals with "the current conditions of national
life." Talk about relevance was probably for the benefit of Congress, which continued to remain skeptical about basic research in
the humanities. As if he felt the need to clear the air, Chairman
Berman said in the *Seventh Annual Report* that "there are many
social issues in which the Endowment does not believe itself obliged
to participate. The most liberal definition of the humanities' interest
must necessarily exclude the determination of public policy."[15]

Yet with regard to the criterion of subject matter, NEH has not
made its position wholly clear, for in the same annual report in

which Berman issued his strictures against weighting in favor of relevance in research proposals, we find, under "Information for Applications," the following: "Applicants in all fields should note that the National Council on the Humanities has placed continuing emphasis on proposals that have bearing on contemporary public problems."[16] Recently NEH has gone even further to signal its interest in proposals relevant to the current conditions of national life. On its standard application form there is a box labeled "Public issues of project, if any," and in the accompanying instructions applicants are asked to "identify any such issue that will be addressed, *e.g.*, aging, religion, death, population growth, urban problems, etc." This absurd farrago of "issues," in combination with the remark "if any," suggests that the information, assuming that it is recorded at all by NEH, serves one purpose only: to persuade Congress that the agency is interested in applied humanistic research.

Most professional humanists will probably be reassured to learn that these expressions of interest in "public issues" mean nothing, that proposals to do applied research in the humanities are not given any special attention in the review process. Indeed, it may well be that applications to do research on supposedly relevant questions actually have a tougher time getting a high rating from professional humanists, since presumably they are on the lookout for the ploy of relevance. Nevertheless, the mere expression of interest in relevance as a funding criterion is both puzzling and disturbing. First, the issues used as examples for the benefit of applicants make little sense. Are religion and death "contemporary issues"? Second, if Congress comes to believe that NEH is less interested in relevance than it professes itself to be, then it is likely to question NEH's good faith on this matter. On the other hand, if Congress does take NEH's profession of interest in applied humanistic research at face value, then NEH is raising expectations it cannot fulfill. Finally, NEH has an obligation to be as open as possible about the review process, yet it is clearly misleading applicants when it implies that projects centering on public issues may fare better than others, since the criterion of relevant subject matter has actually carried little weight in NEH's programs to advance humanistic knowledge.

NEH's support for research in the humanities is channeled through two divisions: the Division of Fellowships and Seminars and the Division of Research. The first of these divisions, which actually allocates only about two-thirds of its funds to programs that support research in the humanities, is divided into six program areas: Fellowships for Independent Study and Research, Fellowships for College Teachers, Summer Stipends for College and University Teachers, Summer Seminars for College Teachers, Summer Seminars for Secondary School Teachers, and Fellowship Support to Centers for Advanced Study.

The second division, Research, funds more ambitious projects, those requiring the expertise of not one but a group of scholars and lasting for a year or more. This division also supports the preparation of research tools and reference works such as dictionaries, encyclopedias, atlases, linguistic grammars, and descriptive catalogs, and funds projects aimed at making primary research resources more readily accessible. The Research Division contains other programs as well; under the rubric of General Research, there are three program areas (Basic Research, Research Conferences, and State, Local, and Regional Studies), while within the Research Materials category lie four more program areas (Research Tools and Reference Works, Editions, Translations, and Publications). Additional program areas entitled Research Resources and Intercultural Research provide funds for national research agencies that, in turn, solicit applications from scholars for work abroad. Finally, the Humanities, Science, and Technology program supports projects that bring the resources and perspectives of the humanities to bear upon science and technology. Each of these many program areas runs its own grant competition, so that applications compete only against other applications in the same category.

The National Science Foundation also divides its support of research into many different categories, but for the most part these categories are organized around scientific disciplines or clusters of related disciplines, so that, for instance, under the general auspices of Mathematical and Physical Sciences there are program areas in Mathematical Sciences, Computer Science, Physics, Chemistry, and Materials Research. The underlying rationale for NEH's multiplicity of program areas is less obvious. Several program areas are defined by subject matter, so that in one program, for example, applications are accepted only from those proposing to do research in state, local, or regional history. Other areas are defined by their applicants; the Fellowship Division's Fellowships for College Teachers program, to name but one, accepts applications only from those teaching at colleges or universities without doctoral programs in the humanities.

Some of the categories of support are intended to promote teaching rather than scholarship—for example, the Summer Seminars for Secondary School Teachers—and would seem to belong in the Education Division. Yet sorting out the different categories is less important than asking the more general question: Why so many categories of support? NEH's continuing desire to reassure Congress that humanistic research is relevant to the national interest has manifestly affected the way it has structured some of its categories of support. They are restrictive according to subject matter, so that only certain kinds of proposals are entertained in each. Within the confines of a particular category, merit may be the primary criterion for awarding a research grant, but the categories themselves give proposals focusing on certain subjects a better competitive chance than they would have if they were to compete in broad categories without such restrictions. To put it another way, a professional humanist submitting a proposal on a particular subject has a better chance of getting an award when the competition is limited to proposals on that subject than if it were open to all subjects. Restrictive categories of support in effect "protect" proposals in each category, since it is highly unlikely that any category will, as it were, come up empty, with reviewers declining to recommend any applications for funding. The existence of restrictive categories, then, makes it likely that grants will be awarded in each, yet it may be that these grants are poorer examples of scholarship in the national interest than applications in the general research category, the unrestrictive category, which have been turned down owing to insufficient funds. In the end, insofar as restrictive categories of support take away funds from general research, they make it less likely that NEH will be supporting the best proposals it receives.

A restrictive category of support is justifiable only if it is clear that the national interest requires the encouragement of proposals in that category. By encouraging proposals in such categories, NEH is to some degree shaping the world of humanistic research, for in essence it is choosing which kinds of research are important enough for special categories of support. It is perfectly legitimate for NEH to formulate such policies, since its enabling legislation directs the agency to develop "a national policy of support for the humanities." Yet NEH has always claimed that it does not consider itself an active shaper of the world of humanistic research, and NEH officials say that they try "to discern rather than define" what is in the national interest.

Why, then, has NEH decided to "highlight" certain fields? As the National Commission on Research has said, "Agencies should endeavor to develop and make explicit relevant policy considerations that are taken into account in judging between proposals and particularly in deciding which research to support among high ranking proposals."[17] Before setting up restrictive—and thereby protective—categories of support for humanistic research, NEH should consult with leading professional humanists to see if they think such categories are necessary. And if it does decide to set up a restrictive category, NEH should publish its reasons for doing so.

In sum, NEH has played somewhat fast and loose with the criterion of research subject. The mixed bag of so-called public issues in which the agency has expressed interest from time to time suggests that it has given little serious thought to the question of applied humanistic research. And by setting up restrictive categories of support, it has introduced the criterion of subject matter where it generally does not belong—before the review process even begins. By and large, the advancement of humanistic knowledge is best served when the question of which proposals are most in the national interest is debated after all the proposals to advance knowledge have been considered by peer reviewers.

What difference has NEH made to humanistic research in the United States? The question is very difficult to answer. Joseph Duffey once rhapsodized that "public assistance to scholars has led to profound and innovative interpretations of the human condition,"[18] but many, perhaps most, "profound and innovative interpretations" would surely have been accomplished even if NEH had never existed. According to William May, a professor of religious studies at Indiana University, "The massive withdrawal of federal money from the sciences would be a catastrophe; from the humanities, it would be an inconvenience, but the research would go on."[19]

There has been a good deal of loose talk about the needs of scholars in the humanities. Testifying before Congress in 1967, Barnaby Keeney declared that "the 2,000-plus serious inquiries regarding senior fellowships received to date . . . demonstrate the critical needs which [NEH] can meet."[20] But surely "serious inquiries," or even full-fledged applications, do not "demonstrate need"; they merely reveal interest in the fact that money is available to free scholars from the time-consuming duties of teaching. Some scholars, to be sure, are needier than others. The plight of younger "gypsy scholars," for instance, is well known; the National Center for Educational Statistics estimates that 15 to 30 percent of all junior faculty members move from one job to another each year.[21] Most of these gypsy scholars are in the humanities. More often than not burdened with heavy course loads and forced constantly to scour the job market, these young scholars (who often teach at colleges without research libraries) have little time to devote to research. Their needs are obviously much greater than those, for instance, of tenured scholars at major research-oriented institutions.

At leading universities, scholars are paid to do research as well as to teach, yet even scholars at these institutions may need funds for travel to research libraries, archives, museums, or archaeological sites. Moreover, large-scale research projects—compiling an encyclopedia or editing someone's papers—are not ordinarily accomplished without financial support, since such work requires not only collaboration among scholars but also the help of research assistants and secretaries. A case in point is the editing and publication of the papers of the Founding Fathers: Franklin, Washington, Adams, Jefferson, Hamilton, and Madison. Preparing these editions has been a slow, expensive process that has required, among other things, long initial searches for materials in libraries, archives, and private collections both here and abroad. The preparation of these editions has been supported by a combination of federal and private funds, but in recent years the federal government's share of the cost has been steadily reduced. NEH has provided a significant amount of support for some editions, but most has come from the National Historical Publications and Records Commission, administered by the National Archives. Edmund S. Morgan, professor of history at Yale University, has stated that "if any kind of historical enterprise

deserves the support of Americans, this one does."[22] In its support
of editions, dictionaries, encyclopedias, and atlases, then, NEH has
had a significant impact, for it is unlikely that these works would
have been produced without the agency's support. NEH also has
made a difference in a broader area of scholarly publication, its
Publications program having in 1982 given more than $420,000 to
scholarly presses for the publication of manuscripts, many of which
were the result of NEH grants. In all likelihood some of these manuscripts would not have been published without the subvention.

There is another area in which NEH could make a difference but
has refrained so far from doing so: graduate support for outstanding
future scholars in the humanities. The 1970s saw the beginning of
what promises to be a long decline in the number of teaching jobs
available to scholars entering the profession. According to William
Bowen, president of Princeton University, the lack of jobs will have
a major impact on the composition and quality of those going on
to graduate study. It is quite possible, according to Bowen, that "the
quality of teaching and research in this country will diminish and
entire fields of knowledge may be weakened for extended periods
of time."[23] A number of concerned observers have called for more
graduate fellowships in the humanities, and not long ago the Andrew W. Mellon Foundation instituted a $25 million humanities fel-
lowship program to be administered by the Woodrow Wilson National Fellowship Foundation.

NSF has had a graduate fellowship program since 1952, and in
1981 it awarded 1,593 fellowships and traineeships, expending $14
million. Edward A. Knapp, who became the director of NSF in
1982, favors continued NSF support for graduate fellowships, which
he terms "absolutely essential."[24] Why has NEH never awarded fellowships for graduate study in the humanities? The main reason has
been the opinion of Senator Pell, who has been strongly opposed
to such a program. In 1970, for example, Pell expressed apprehen-
sion, at NEH's reauthorization hearings, "that the humanities program might get too much into the esoteric field, supporting post-
doctoral studies, and even helping graduate students through their
doctorates."[25] In June 1983, however, the House Appropriations
subcommittee responsible for NEH's appropriations recommended
that $5 million of NEH's budget be used to provide $11,000-a-year

fellowships for outstanding graduate students in the humanities. Each scholar would receive $7,000 in living expenses and $4,000 for tuition.

NEH should support graduate students in the humanities in order to ensure a continuity of humanistic scholarship, but the issue of whether a greater proportion of NEH's budget should be allocated to humanistic research is not quite so clear. Some observers worry that increases in NEH support for research might dry up private support; according to the *1980 Report*, "the total number of fellowships for research in the humanities leveled off around 1973–74 and has declined since then in the case of some major private sources of support."[26] Duffey declared that "the endowment is now the single most important agency furthering the discovery, analysis, presentation, maintenance, and revision of humanistic knowledge in the nation,"[27] but if private foundations stopped supporting humanistic research, maverick scholars would find it harder to get support for their work. Private foundations can take greater risks, can be open to a wider variety of proposals, than NEH, for the obvious reasons that they are not directly accountable to Congress, but it is unlikely that private foundations make their decisions about what to do (or what not to do) by looking closely at what NEH is doing. In any case, we are unaware of the extent to which private foundations support humanistic research, since no figures have been compiled. Many private foundations indirectly support research by supporting education in general.

In sum, it is as difficult to determine the needs of scholars in the humanities as it is to translate those needs into a specific level of federal support. Are NEH'S funds for research in the humanities too generous, too penurious, or entirely appropriate? We cannot say, but if Congress were to cut NEH's budget for research dramatically, it would be a signal to the academy that Congress does not take seriously NEH's mandate to promote progress and scholarship in the humanities. Humanistic research is admittedly not, for the most part, as essential to the nation as is scientific research, but research—as the *1980 Report* observes—is vital to the humanities.

In any case, speaking so generally about the sciences and the humanities does not help us gauge the relative importance of particular disciplines. Research in some humanistic disciplines may be more important to the nation's well-being than research in some scientific disciplines. International studies, which is less a discipline than a composite of disciplines, is a case in point. In *Politics*, Aristotle observes that "if a polis is to live a political life, not a life of isolation, it is a good thing that its legislator should also pay regard to neighboring countries."[28] In the last quarter of the twentieth century, neighboring countries, at least for a great power like the United States, constitute the whole world. According to a recent report by the President's Commission on Foreign Languages and International Studies, the nation's understanding of the world is "dangerously inadequate." The United States, the report said, "requires far more capacities to communicate with its allies, analyze the behavior of potential adversaries, and earn the trust and sympathies of the uncommitted." And it warned that "nothing less is at issue than the nation's security."[29] Basic research in the history and culture of other nations is thus manifestly in the national interest. Congress thought so as far back as 1958, for in that year it passed the National Defense Education Act, which included more than $60 million for foreign language training and provided a major stimulus to foreign area studies and research.

But the most important consideration is not determining the appropriate level of support for the advancement of humanistic knowledge; neither is it deciding which kinds of support will ensure the continuance of outstanding humanistic research. The most important consideration is ensuring that merit remains the primary consideration when judging applications to do research, for there is no question but that Congress will press NEH to find ways of ensuring a more "representative" distribution of grants. As Duffey himself asked in a recent speech to ACLS: "To what extent should the Endowment . . . seek to distribute its resources more evenly across a broader, more representative range of constituents?"[30] To introduce criteria other than merit is certainly appropriate at times, but a concern with the distribution of grants makes it unlikely that merit will remain the primary consideration. In its report on *Review Processes*, the National Commission on Research affirmed its support of merit: "The Commission believes that deciding the direction of U.S. science through the open competition of unsolicited proposals, and especially through the selection of proposals through peer review, is of great importance to the success of U.S. science and, therefore, deserves support."[31] If NEH does become concerned with achieving a "representative" distribution of awards to advance humanistic knowledge, then it will no longer be honoring the potential achievement of the nation's "natural aristocrats" in the humanities. And it will be signaling to the academy—and to anyone else who is watching—that it is no longer interested in the advancement of humanistic knowledge.

6

The Problem
of Preservation

DESPITE the proliferation of program areas within the National Endowment for the Humanities, the agency has for the most part taken
a passive role in its support of humanistic research, responding to
applications rather than attempting to influence research by con-
tracting for certain kinds of projects or instituting more and more
restrictive categories of support. When NEH came into existence,
however, both the chairman and the National Council realized that
for the agency to promote progress and scholarship in the humanities it would have to take an active role in several areas. The most
significant of these is undoubtedly the area of public programs, but
the nation's libraries, especially research libraries, also demand active involvement on the part of NEH. The agency was well aware
from its inception of some significant problems facing research libraries; the *Second Annual Report* bemoans the fact that, although
"research in the humanities requires access to its materials, . . .
many . . . collections are uncatalogued or insufficiently organized." [1]

We have seen that the needs of scholars in the mid-1960s were
not as evident as some spokesmen for the humanities claimed, but
the needs of research libraries were quite obvious. The essay "Libraries for the Humanities," coauthored by the directors of several
major American research libraries and published in the *1964 Report*,
stressed the vital importance of libraries to scholarly research and
drew attention to the significant problems besetting them. Noting
that the library resources at a scholar's disposal "affect both the
direction and the quality of his research," the authors of this doc-

ument declared that libraries "ought to have a particularly important place in any broad program for support of the humanities." In particular, libraries needed help in dealing with two major problems. First, major research libraries "are [now] so large that it is increasingly difficult for them to make their holdings readily accessible and to respond effectively to changing needs." And second, these institutions "now realize that a large percentage of the volumes on their shelves . . . are disintegrating physically at an alarming rate."[2]

Have research libraries in fact had a "particularly important place" in NEH's support of the humanities? Judging from remarks in the *1980 Report*, NEH has apparently done relatively little to help these institutions, which appear to have been in even worse straits in 1980 than they were in 1965. According to the *1980 Report*, the deterioration of books "is a massive national problem threatening to reduce to dust within our lifetime perhaps half of the 227 million volumes held by research libraries."[3] It is not only books that are in danger of deteriorating; there are serious problems with the preservation of photographs, microfilm, video cassettes, records, and videotapes as well. Several years ago, for example, a fire at the National Archives destroyed millions of feet of historic film. The *1980 Report* also warns that "the sheer volume of research threatens to inundate libraries, scholars, students, and the reading public with unmanageable masses of printed matter." This veritable explosion "raises urgent questions of what shall be published and purchased, how it shall be stored, and who shall read it."[4]

The *1980 Report* has not been alone in drawing attention to the plight of research libraries in recent years. In a report entitled *Scholarly Communication*, the National Enquiry into Scholarly Communication observed that librarians in the major research centers are "facing the difficult task of allocating increasingly scarce dollars among the vast and steadily growing numbers of books, journals, microforms, and other materials of scholarship." This rapid growth, the report noted, "means that each library is becoming increasingly less able to satisfy the research and educational needs of its users."[5] A report by the Association of Research Libraries showed that operating expenses in member libraries have doubled in the past decade; expenditures for library materials increased 91 percent, while the number of volumes acquired decreased by 22.5 percent.[6] And the director of the Council on Library Resources has recently pointed out that "the sheer size of . . . collections, which have tended to double every fifteen or twenty years during much of this century, has made all operations more difficult."[7]

Broadly speaking, the problem research libraries face is both technical—how to preserve materials from deterioration—and what Daniel Boorstin terms epistemological, involving the "question of priorities or techniques of selecting what is to be preserved."[8] Research libraries, then, are burdened with both the need to preserve materials from destruction and the equally pressing need to decide what to preserve, given the virtual impossibility of preserving everything. Archives as well as research libraries have been overwhelmed by the explosive growth of materials in the postwar era, a growth that has entailed a staggering financial burden and that has forced librarians to turn to scholars in the humanities for an answer to the question of what should be preserved.

In the opinion of a number of knowledgeable observers, these problems of preservation should be addressed by NEH. Testifying before Congress in 1981, Barbara Tuchman and Justin Kaplan declared that NEH should aid research libraries. According to Kaplan, "our libraries and their melancholy inventories of lost, stolen, mutilated, and worn-out books symbolize the general situation of the humanities in the time of rising costs and shrinking budgets."[9] And the *1980 Report* argued that "preservation . . . may indeed be the most important and least risky investment the federal government can make in our national culture."[10] In recent years NEH has come to a similar conclusion. In a report submitted to Congress in 1980, Chairman Duffey stated: "Perhaps no area of the humanities presents a stronger case for increased support than research libraries, archives, and other collections of research materials," adding that "a most compelling area of need is the conservation and preservation of documentary resources."[11]

These remarks imply that NEH had previously done little to address the needs of research libraries, and it is true that during the first decade of its existence the agency paid scant attention to them, although in 1972 it did offer a challenge grant to the financially beleaguered New York Public Library. According to NEH's *Seventh Annual Report*, the Research Division "undertook no single action of more importance in fiscal 1972 than helping to keep open the mammoth collections of [this] library,"[12] which is unique in that it is both a public library and one of the world's major research libraries. The terms of the grant were generous: NEH would match every private dollar raised by the library with one federal dollar, up to a limit of $500,000. In subsequent years the formula was altered, with NEH offering only one federal dollar for every two private dollars. But the New York Public Library has done its part of the fund-raising job well; since 1972 it has been awarded approximately $12 million in federal matching funds, which means that it has itself raised approximately $24 million from the private sector. Both this series of grants and others to research libraries, either challenge grants or awards for specific projects, have indirectly helped them deal with the preservation problem by enabling them to achieve a better financial footing. These funds help libraries meet general operating expenses rather than pay for preservation projects, but many libraries consider preservation costs as part of their operating expenses—for example, the New York Public Library, which runs one of the most extensive microfilming operations in the country. Such grants have also enabled a number of research libraries to broaden their constituencies so that they could tap more sources in their fund-raising.

In the early 1970s NEH awarded a few grants to research libraries to help them cope with organizing their collections, but it was not until the mid-1970s that the agency set up a special category of support under which research libraries and archives could apply for grants to "improve the ways in which librarians, archivists, and others care for and make available the research materials entrusted to them."[13] Much of the credit for establishing this program area, called Research Collections before its name was changed to Research Resources, should go to the research libraries themselves, especially to the Independent Research Libraries Association (IRLA), which began to lobby intensively for NEH support in the early 1970s. At the 1973 reauthorization hearings, representatives from the IRLA presented a strong case for NEH support, arguing that since research libraries are not appendages of any university or other institution, they receive neither institutional funding from universities (as university libraries do) nor public funds from taxpayers (as public libraries do). Their chief spokesman was Lawrence W. Towner, director of the Newberry Library in Chicago, which had already received several grants from NEH. Towner let it be known that, in the case of his own library as well as of other members of the IRLA, "the National Endowment has become crucial to our effective operation in meeting the growing opportunities to serve . . . . We need funds for almost every aspect of our operations—acquisitions, binding, conservation, construction, fellowships, and publications. Most of these we expect to raise in a carefully orchestrated combination of local support and grants from national foundations. But our ability to do so will be greatly enhanced by the judicious support on select occasions by the National Endowment for the Humanities."[14] To a question from Senator Pell about the specific needs of independent as well as other research libraries, Towner replied: "If I had to single out [one] overwhelming need . . . I think it would be to conserve what we already have." He explained that "we are facing a crisis of major proportions . . . because of the deterioration of our books and manuscripts, due to several causes . . . . Therefore we all need to give very serious consideration to major restoration and conservation projects."[15]

But Towner's plea was not quickly heeded by NEH. Although Research Resources soon became a program area with a substantial amount of funding (in 1977 it made eighty-seven awards totaling $3.5 million in outright funds and $5.1 million in gift and matching funds), the Conservation and Preservation Program was not established until 1981. In that year it expended approximately $500,000 for nine projects.

Although it took NEH a long time to address the question of preservation, the 1981 date for the formal establishment of a preservation program is to some degree misleading, for NEH had been making grants in this area for several years. In 1980 Duffey testified before Congress that, "with Endowment grants, dozens of collections of books have been catalogued and archival materials of all kinds have been organized, have been put in acid-free folders and protective containers to ensure their preservation, and have had finding aids prepared so that scholars and others can use them."[16] But clearly NEH had not addressed the twofold problem of preservation in the way that Towner had recommended. Duffey himself implied as much, pointing out during his testimony that NEH "has insufficient funds to tackle problems of this magnitude, but has made grants for model projects."[17]

"Insufficient funds" is not a satisfactory explanation for NEH's long delay in addressing the preservation dilemma. Research libraries had long been in dire straits, and if they were as important to progress and scholarship in the humanities as most spokesmen for the humanities—including Duffey—claimed, then NEH should have transferred funds from other areas early on in order to increase its support for research libraries. At the very least, the agency might have sponsored conferences on the question. But until Duffey lingered pointedly over the importance of research libraries in his testimony before Congress in 1980, no NEH chairman had singled out the problem for attention. Duffey's pet project, as we have seen, was social history, and Berman prided himself on successes in public programming. In short, it is safe to say that in the first fifteen years of NEH's history the twofold problem of preservation was neglected.

There were several reasons for this neglect, one of which was NEH's preoccupation with addressing the concerns of Senator Pell. Pell was not hostile to the idea of alleviating the plight of research libraries; in response to Towner's testimony he warned that "we will have no cultural legacy unless there is some way it can be preserved." He had even spoken of setting up a National Institute of Conservation "with perhaps a portion of it devoted to paper conservation."[18] But Senator Pell's main concern, as we have seen, was neither research libraries nor research in general; he had always wanted NEH's funds to have as much impact as possible on the general public.

He did not, of course, always get what he wanted. So many of his suggestions were ignored that a note of peevishness occasionally crept into his comments. In 1979, for instance, he complained: "I continue to press the idea that people who are not related to the academic community but have an interest in the humanities should receive small individual grants."[19] But even though NEH failed to act on some of Pell's suggestions, it felt obliged to appease him as much as possible during the 1970s, which meant finding new ways of instituting public programs in the humanities. In the process of increasing its budget for public programs, thus proving to Pell that it was not wedded to the academy, NEH was reluctant to ask for increased support for projects that could not be construed as public programs. The agency could, and did, boast of its support for the New York Public Library, a major public institution as well as a research library, but its movement into the area of preservation was slowed, at least in part, by the fact that mounting a big effort in this area was unlikely to win NEH what Pell called "greater visibility."

Another possible reason for NEH's reluctance to address the problem of preservation was its fear of embarking upon projects that might overlap those of other federal agencies. This fear was understandable, since NEH was often questioned about the extent to which its work might duplicate that of other agencies. As Joseph Duffey asserted in 1978: "If we fail to make a clear, common statement of public purpose for our mission, then the case for the National Endowment for the Humanities will appear unnecessarily vague and confusing to Congress, which today is understandably concerned about possible overlaps with other agencies, such as the Arts Endowment, Museum Services Institute, the Corporation for Public Broadcasting, and the Office of Education."[20]

Thus there existed the possibility that NEH-supported projects focusing on preservation might overlap with those sponsored by the Library of Congress, whose own office of preservation had a budget of $5 million for preservation research in 1982. Organized in 1965 in response to a report that drew attention to the "staggering dimensions" of the preservation problem, this office, which now employs 135 persons,[21] is engaged in a variety of projects. In July 1982, for instance, it began large-scale testing of a chemical-vapor process making it possible to remove acid, the cause of paper's deterioration, from the pages of books, rendering them relatively immune to decay. By 1985 the Library of Congress hopes to have built its own facility to take page-crumbling acid out of 500,000 books a year.[22]

Perhaps because it was worried about overlap, NEH was slow to become actively involved in seeking out preservation projects. In recent years, however, it has definitely expanded its efforts in this area. It has supported certification programs that train preservation administrators and paper conservators (those who actually preserve paper). In 1982, moreover, NEH gave a grant of $949,000 to six institutions for the preservation of American newspapers. The project, entitled the United States Newspaper Program, will develop a computerized databank that eventually will make accessible the contents of more than 300,000 newspapers published in the United States since 1690. Researchers will have access to them through terminals located at more than 2,000 centers across the nation.

The projects that NEH has sponsored to date have rarely focused on the epistemological problem of preservation. This is unfortunate because, according to an observer writing in the *New York Times*, "the central problem faced by librarians [today] is what to save, since clearly the technology is not yet at hand that will permit them to save everything."[23] The agency has obviously neglected this problem, yet we cannot place the blame at NEH's doorstep when scholars in the humanities have neglected it as well. According to Daniel Boorstin, the twofold problem of preservation "is the great forgotten problem of our age. It has been forgotten, not by specialists and librarians but, to a surprising extent, by scholars, men of affairs, and those who use the materials of civilization."[24] The main reason why the question has not been more seriously addressed by NEH is that humanistic scholars themselves have been loath to confront it.

Some historians, exacerbating the epistemological problem, believe that everything should be saved. At a recent conference on the Research, Use and Disposition of Senators' Papers, one scholar did acknowledge that the sheer bulk of modern records constituted a problem not only for the historian but also for the taxpayer. After conceding that Congress might legitimately decide that the cost of preserving certain records was simply too high, he was still reluctant to admit that anything should be destroyed. He said he was bothered "by talk of destroying large quantities of constituent mail . . . . If we are going to understand not only our local history, but also our political culture, that is to say, that part of our culture that springs not from the pages of the *Washington Post* or the *Congressional Record*, then I think we are overlooking a most valuable source if we capriciously destroy these."[25] Another scholar at the same conference readily admitted his "interest in preserving every single piece of paper" because he did not want "to be in the position of having to decide what questions future historians will ask and what they will need."[26]

The defenders of total preservation often imply that the proliferation of historical materials helps to increase our understanding of the past. In his introduction to *The Past Before Us: Contemporary Historical Writing in the United States*, Michael Kammen states that "as vast amounts of primary and secondary source material accumulate, . . . we realize that familiar explanatory frames of reference have broken down and cease to explain the past adequately."[27] There are historians, however, who question whether the profusion of materials will truly aid the historian. J.H. Hexter has attacked those who, like Alice's White Knight, are "excessively concerned . . . to be 'provided with everything.'" Far from being adequately equipped for the quest for historical truth, Hexter said, these historians "often seem engulfed in useless clutter."[28] And William Leuchtenberg, a professor of history at the University of North Carolina, has advised historians to "confront the fact that not every piece of paper that comes out of Congress from now until eternity is going to be maintained . . . . I don't believe that in the end it is really going to further historical research. And I don't think we can call upon the American people to support that kind of expenditure." Although Leuchtenberg acknowledged that the special interests of social historians should be taken into account, he also cautioned colleagues not to "kid [them]selves about what the likelihood is of the use of the kinds of materials that are now being generated."[28] Barbara Tuchman has complained that the preoccupation with preserving everything has resulted in the "survival of trivia of appalling proportions."[30]

Faced with the practical problems inherent in storing such a volume of material, research librarians and archivists are inclined to be impatient with historians bent on preserving everything. Daniel Reed, director of the Presidential Libraries program of the National Archives, has lamented that "many of us who are charged with the custody of large bodies of important papers are actually in a situation where we cannot bring in the next truck load unless we get something out of the building first." Despite its budget of $80 million, the National Archives "simply cannot afford to keep everything against every possible use." The cost of space is only one consideration, according to Reed. "There is also the matter of all the man-hours . . . for the processing, arranging, and making usable a body of material."[31] He pointed out that it was highly unlikely that Congress would appropriate sufficient funds to enable the National Archives to preserve everything some historians would like to see preserved.

Scholars in the humanities have paid little attention to the plight of archivists and research librarians. According to James Banner, chairman of the now-defunct American Association for the Advancement of the Humanities (AAAH), "humanists have done comparatively little to support the research libraries upon which they depend." Proposing the creation of a joint committee consisting of the AAAH, the Association of Research Libraries, and the Independent Research Libraries Association, Banner warned that "what is at stake . . . is the very foundation of our intellectual culture and our access to knowledge."[32]

NEH could undoubtedly have done more to bring the question of preservation to the attention of scholars in the humanities, but its failure to do so is understandable, since the question was of little interest to Congress and was also surrounded by controversy. In 1970 the American Historical Association issued a report advising scholars to take the "initiative in developing a rational program of preservation, which should be altered periodically as changing interests and circumstances require." It called upon the historian, archivist, and curator to "find ways to preserve a rationally determined sample of this material."[33] But what is rational to some historians (or archivists or curators) will of course be irrational to others. Although it is doubtful that scholars in the humanities will ever reach a consensus on the question of what to preserve, by wrestling with it they may be able to offer some guidance to beleaguered research librarians and archivists. As the president of the Council on Library Resources has urged: "It is important that library users—especially humanists, for whom research libraries are absolutely essential—join forces with research librarians to guide the course of change."[34]

In recent years, the problem of preservation has become more acute not only because it has been neglected but also because the blossoming subdiscipline of social history has increased the kinds of materials that, according to social historians, research libraries need to preserve. It would be unfair to single out NEH as the government agency most responsible for the proliferation of materials to be preserved; both social history and another new specialty, oral history, would no doubt have flourished without NEH support. The problem, as John Hope Franklin has pointed out, is much larger than NEH. "During the last two decades, the activities of government at every level . . . [have done] much to set the stage for an acceleration of historical activities in the United States."[35] Within the last fifteen years the federal government has greatly increased its support for cultural production of many kinds—films, records, tapes, books, and articles.

NEH can do nothing about the generation of materials, yet it can support, or even implement, projects that may help scholars, archivists, and librarians to arrive at selective collection policies. Such policies would enable research libraries and archives to hold down their general operating costs, since "the acquisition, processing, and maintenance of materials" are what generate the bulk of such costs.[36]

NEH is only one of a number of federal agencies that provide support for research libraries and deal with the problem of preservation. The Department of Education, for example, incorporates a library program that allocates $6 million a year to research libraries to aid in building and conserving collections. In 1981 the Reagan administration proposed to eliminate not only the $6 million for research libraries but the Department of Education's entire budget of $80 million for all libraries. The administration also proposed large cuts in the budget of the National Archives, which administers the National Historical Publications and Records Commission. Congress ultimately rejected the administration's proposals, but they provoked discussion about the amount of federal support appropriate not only for the National Archives but for research libraries as well.

The authors of a 1970 report by the American Historical Association asserted that the federal government should "commit itself . . . to the maintenance and promotion of the nation's research libraries as a national resource."[37] Many observers have agreed with them. Testifying recently before Congress, for instance, Barbara Tuchman argued that to reduce the National Archives' program funds by 30 percent, the amount proposed by the Reagan administration, would be "sheer destruction, because continuing records of government agencies cannot be accessioned, catalogued, or properly housed."[38] Few people can be found who oppose all federal support to the nation's major research libraries, which, in the view of James Thorpe, the director of the Huntington Library, are national treasures deserving "national recognition and support."[39]

These affirmations of the need for federal support do not, however, address the difficult question of how much support is justified.

A report from the National Enquiry into Scholarly Communication recognized that there are limits to the amount of data that the nation can afford to preserve, yet it also noted that, since "the private marketplace cannot be relied upon to produce the socially optimal amount of such public goods, . . . subsidies of one form or another are generally required."[40] Is it possible to translate the notion of a "socially optimal amount" of knowledge into dollars and cents?

To date, the task has not been accomplished, and debate continues over an appropriate level of support for research libraries as well as the National Archives. It seems clear that to cut the budget of the National Archives would be ill advised. Commenting on the possible firing of 130 Archives employees, *Humanities Report* noted that "the arduous work of gathering federal documents, deciding what is worth saving and what can be disposed of, and organizing, declassifying, and providing access to such documents . . . will all be severely hampered."[41] The growth of the Archives has been impressive—from 136,743 cubic feet of stored material in 1938 to an astronomical 1,369,707 cubic feet in 1981. The loss of trained personnel would obviously make it exceedingly difficult for the staff to oversee the collections already in the Archives, especially to make sure these materials do not deteriorate, and would make it equally difficult to effect a collection policy that would reduce the rate of growth in the amount of materials, for such a policy requires a relatively large and thoroughly trained staff.

It would also be unwise to cut the budget of the Department of Education's Library Programs, since libraries in general are in serious financial straits and have become dependent upon such funds to meet increased operating costs, most notably the high costs of works published as parts of continuing series, especially scholarly journals. In the long run, however, the nation's research libraries may be better able to withstand such cuts than the National Archives; they are less labor-intensive than archives, since much of their work revolves around rendering materials accessible, a task that lends itself well to technological innovation. Moreover, research libraries can cut costs by sharing resources.[42] All the major research libraries are already moving in the direction of shared collection development. In 1974 the Research Libraries Group (RLG), a national consortium of twenty-nine libraries, was formed to share bibliographic information and to provide patrons access to materials owned by cooperating institutions. It now attempts to coordinate its own acquisitions with those of other member libraries. Members of RLG have cooperated also on preservation projects. In 1983 NEH and the Andrew W. Mellon Foundation each awarded $675,000 to RLG for a cooperative preservation microfilming program in which seven institutions will microfilm monographs, U.S. imprints, and Americana from their collections. They plan to select materials published between 1876 and 1900, a period when most publications were printed on highly acidic paper that has become too brittle for the materials to be maintained in their original form.

Some research librarians have questioned the wisdom of seeking extensive federal support. Richard De Gennaro, director of libraries at the University of Pennsylvania, has commented that "the more I observe the workings of the federal government, the more convinced I become that the solutions to our research problems are not to be found primarily in Washington, but in the voluntary and concrete actions of a peer group of research libraries with a common need and a common interest in solving those problems." According to De Gennaro, librarians need to "re-examine and re-assess their traditional attitudes . . . and adopt positions that are more in tune with the economic and technical realities of the electronic information age we are now entering."[43]

De Gennaro was alluding to the revolutionary changes in techniques for storing and disseminating knowledge that are the products of new technologies, changes that, as one observer put it, are comparable to those wrought by the invention of the printing press. If data compression techniques continue on their present curve, it will be possible by the late 1980s to store cumbersome books entirely on microchips, and a whole library in a space about the size of one of today's paperbacks.

The ultimate extent to which technological innovation will transform the research library is still a matter of debate. Yet virtually all observers acknowledge that innovation will take place and that the problem for most research libraries will be to find the money to pay for technological changes. An observer in *Humanities Report* summed up the problem this way: "If research libraries find it increasingly difficult to obtain minimal funding for current operations from their universities, it may be difficult for library directors to persuade hard-pressed administrations to make large investments in technical systems."[44]

The problems of research libraries are undoubtedly acute, but in many ways so are the problems of other libraries. They, too, face the question of what to preserve—whether to stock only contemporary books and serials or to maintain a collection with some depth. It is probably unwise to attempt to draw a clear distinction between research libraries and general libraries, since research libraries often serve as general libraries—for example, for scholars who want to do some reading in areas outside their own disciplines. All libraries, as New York Public Library director Vartan Gregorian has said, can serve as sources of lifelong education for anyone wanting "to connect with the past."[45]

NEH's role in the affairs of research libraries will necessarily remain limited, but these libraries should be of considerable concern to NEH, for, if they cannot cope with the problem of preservation, progress and scholarship in the humanities will suffer. We cannot say with any confidence that important work in the humanities is being left undone because not enough fellowships are available, but we can say with certainty that many scholars in the humanities (especially those not affiliated with major universities) would find it difficult to pursue their work if the NEH-supported New York Public Library, which spent $1.2 million on book conservation in 1981, were to lose a significant proportion of its holdings through deterioration or could no longer afford to remain a major research library.

7

The Teaching
of the Humanities

WHEN THEY voted for the establishment of the National Endowment for the Humanities, many congressmen were worried about the lack of a balanced education in America. They agreed with the *1964 Report* that, although much has been done to improve the teaching of the sciences, "similar steps have not been taken in the humane studies, so that a student may . . . enter a college or university without adequate training in the humanities or, for that matter, a rudimentary acquaintance with them."[1] The authors of the report recommended a number of programs that would, they hoped, address the problem of teaching at the elementary and secondary levels, but they stressed that a national humanities foundation should "support improved teaching at all levels of education." It should, moreover, encourage "experiments in presentation and organization, including interdisciplinary studies, where many fruitful advances may be made," as well as develop new curricular materials.[2]

As if to stress the interest of the Commission on the Humanities in teaching, the first essay in the *1964 Report*'s extensive appendix was entitled "The Humanities and the Schools." The work of a board composed of prominent educators, including the president of Columbia University Teachers College, the essay painted a gloomy picture of humanistic education in the schools, listing the "lack of properly educated teachers, lack of time, lack of space, and lack of good teaching materials" as the "principal difficulties to be faced," and arguing that "without major efforts . . . the status and influence of the humanities in the schools will inevitably decline in the years ahead." Only the "massive support . . . of a national agency with the resources and leadership to work in all areas of humanistic learning," the essay continued, would prevent such a decline.[3] After eight pages' worth of specific recommendations, the educators concluded by asserting that "a national foundation for the humanities which can support efforts of this kind will greatly advance educational quality in the United States."[4]

In its *First Annual Report*, NEH affirmed its commitment to improving the teaching of the humanities, calling such improvement in schools, colleges, and universities perhaps its most important objective. In 1970, however, Barnaby Keeney informed Congress that the "greatest deficiency" lay in higher education, adding that it would be wise to concentrate on improving postsecondary education, since "what happens there is quickly reflected in the secondary schools."[5] Throughout the 1970s the agency allocated more money for higher than for secondary education, yet it also allocated an increasingly smaller percentage of its total budget to the Education Division. (In 1971 this division received 44 percent of the agency's funds; in 1980, only 16 percent.) This decreasing percentage did not mean that NEH had lost interest in improving the teaching of the humanities; the number of dollars for the Education Division actually increased, but the budgets for Public and State Programs increased more dramatically.

In general, then, NEH has heeded the *1964 Report*: it has tried to improve the teaching of the humanities. But to what effect? "American education," Jessica Tuchman Mathews claimed in a 1981 *Washington Post* article, "is in a fearsome decline."[6] The authors of the *1980 Report* agreed, asserting that "a dramatic improvement in the quality of education in our elementary and secondary schools is the highest educational priority for America in the 1980s."[7] Even officials of NEH agreed with these gloomy assessments. In 1980 Duffey confessed to Congress that "by every available measure, American education in the humanities is experiencing severely troubled times." And in 1981 the director of the Elementary and Secondary Education Program at NEH declared that the present state of education "should shock us."[8]

When observers in the late 1970s and early 1980s bemoaned the dismal state of American education, they were speaking not just of the humanities. Many, including Mathews, argued that the decline was even worse in science and mathematics. According to an article in the *New York Times*, Americans take so few courses in these areas that the country "may be on its way to technological illiteracy—with most of its citizens unable to think and function effectively in an increasingly complex technical society."[9] Fifteen years after NEH was created, American education was balanced, it seemed, only insofar as it was equally weak in the sciences and the humanities.

But we should not rush to assume that NEH is in any way responsible for this sorry fact. While it is possible that the agency abetted the decline, it is also possible that NEH prevented its becoming more acute. Most probably, however, NEH has not been a significant factor in American education one way or the other. In short, its program to improve the teaching of the humanities may have been largely ineffectual.

Gauging the influence of NEH on education is no easy task. For one thing, the agency is only a small voice in the chorus of federal aid to education. And federal aid to education has always been much less than state and local aid. According to Chester E. Finn, Jr., a professor of education and public policy at Vanderbilt University, Washington's share of national spending on elementary and secondary education has never been more than 8 percent of the total.[10] Moreover, federal aid to education has been dominated by the educator rather than the scholar of the humanities. It is difficult to generalize about educators, although it would be fair to say that they are typically well disposed toward educational innovation, often preoccupied with pedagogy, and usually less interested in the content than in the goals of the curriculum. We hear the educator's voice in a Carnegie Commission report stressing the need for colleges and universities to "encourage innovation and flexibility," and again, in a second Carnegie Commission report, stating that "the campus can and should be an ethically stimulating environment."[11]

As one would expect, this voice has predominated in the Department of Education. We hear it in the enabling legislation of the National Institute of Education, which mandates that the institute "advance the practice of education, as an art, science, and profession."[12] It appears again in a brochure put out by the Fund for the Improvement of Postsecondary Education (FIPSE), which was mandated by Congress to support "the reform, innovation, and improvement of postsecondary education." FIPSE, according to this brochure, remains "committed to the goal of improvement and to the principle of learner-centeredness as an important characteristic of all projects we support," and believes that "renewing educational content is at the heart of postsecondary education."[13] Intent, during the past fifteen years, on reforming the curriculum and devising new methodologies to improve teaching, not only in the humanities but also in other areas of the curriculum, educators have solicited federal support from a number of government agencies. In 1974, for example, more than twenty-five separate federal agencies channeled money into higher education.

What have the educators wrought? According to Finn, "the U.S. Education Department has done practically nothing to foster higher school standards or better teaching."[14] J. Myron Atkin, dean of the School of Education at Stanford University, argues that "government initiatives in curriculum may have contributed not only to a loss of teacher autonomy, but also to a narrowing of [the] range of [teachers'] technical as well as curricular responsibilities. . . . Government attention—while it will improve certain conditions in the education system—is likely to contribute in direct, subtle, and unintended ways to a redefinition of schooling and professional practice that itself will lead . . . to further decline."[15] And David G. Savage, associate editor of *Education U.S.A.*, accuses federal aid to education of having "created a new class of bureaucrats, paper pushers, compliance officers, grant writers and lobbyists."[16]

According to many observers, federal programs tend to reward those who are preoccupied with innovation, with reforming the curriculum. The overall effect of such efforts, regardless of the quality of individual funded projects, may be negative because they encourage innovation for its own sake. Daniel L. Duke of Stanford University's School of Education finds that "very few projects are funded because they promise to implement an established program or replicate a practice of proven worth. Money goes to those who propose unique solutions to problems. New ideas—or old ideas carefully designed to appear new—capture the imagination of funding agencies. . . . By exclusively valuing that which appears to be new, those who seek to encourage the improvement of education actually devalue the successes of the past."[17]

In the view of David Savage, "the federal government has sought to do too much in education . . . which has resulted in a fractured, faddish school curriculum."[18] The authors of the *1980 Report* agree. "The curriculum is fragmented," they believe, "partly because government policy has encouraged a proliferation of subjects and has required schools to fulfill many specialized responsibilities."[19] Fundamental subjects such as history, English, and foreign languages have lost ground as a result. Efforts to reform the curriculum have also tended to lower the morale of teachers, with those of acknowledged excellence often slighted by educational administrators in favor of those who are adept at getting grants.

NEH, too, has bowed before the god of innovation. Although the section on the Education Division in the *Eighth Annual Report* reminded readers that "the uses of imagination are not limited to innovation," in 1980 the division's director boasted that NEH "has helped shape a garden of new courses" while aiding in the flowering of "whole new fields."[20] Yet because NEH relies less on the judgments of educators than on those of scholars in the humanities, it should be regarded as a dissident voice in the federal educational bureaucracy. And insofar as NEH is concerned with the curriculum rather than with pedagogy—with texts rather than students—it may have been a force for good. It is difficult to come to a general conclusion about the effect of NEH on the teaching of the humanities because NEH is primarily a grant-making agency, one that does not prescribe remedies for education but rather awards grants to particular proposals that in most cases have not been solicited by the agency. For the most part NEH reflects rather than shapes the climate of opinion in the world of humanistic education.

Still, since NEH is empowered to formulate a "national policy" to aid progress in the humanities, it is appropriate for the agency to take an active role in the world of humanistic education. This can be accomplished in several ways. First, its chairman can call attention to weaknesses in the teaching of the humanities, or, more broadly, can speak out in behalf of rigorous humanistic education. Second, NEH can do much to influence education simply by means of its general guidelines and categories of support, which can be used to encourage certain kinds of applications or applications in particular disciplines. In 1982, for example, Richard Ekman, director of the Education Division, promised not only that the division's new guidelines would "eliminate exclusive support of innovation" but also that the division would soon introduce a new category of grants to help colleges increase the effectiveness of introductory courses in the humanities by ensuring that they be taught by the best teachers.[21] Finally, both the chairman and the staff of NEH can informally encourage certain kinds of proposals or invite leading scholars to submit proposals, even though they cannot, of course, guarantee that these proposals will be funded.

To a degree, then, NEH can attempt to influence the teaching of the humanities. Certainly it has tried to do so in the past. But how influential has it been? Perhaps the best way to answer this question is to look at some specific areas of the curriculum. In 1978 Robert Lumiansky, president of the American Council of Learned Societies, remarked that

> to indulge ourselves at this point with high-flown talk about
> "reaffirming humanistic values" would be a waste of time.
> What we need first is effective attention devoted to the basic
> humanistic disciplines in our public educational systems, cur-
> rently in great disarray. Those disciplines, as I see it, are three:
> 1) written and oral communication in the English language; 2)
> history, broadly defined; and 3) foreign languages. Unless we
> can raise substantially the general level of ability in these areas,
> we do not stand much chance of securing for the humanities
> a greatly expanded role in our national life.[22]

By examining the history of NEH's efforts to deal with these "basic humanistic disciplines," we may be able to discover whether or not the agency has paid them "effective attention."

FOREIGN LANGUAGES

Most observers agreed with Lumiansky that the teaching of writing and history needed to be improved, yet most also singled out foreign language instruction as the most pressing problem—a problem that had resulted in a serious shortage of American experts on most areas of the world. The *1964 Report* paid little attention to this problem. In the section entitled "The Humanities and the Schools," history and English were cited as two areas of the curriculum where reform was necessary; no mention was made of foreign languages. The Modern Language Association (MLA), in an appendix to the report, claimed that the teaching of foreign languages had improved owing to its own Foreign Language Program launched in 1952. "Students entering college today," the MLA noted, "are much better prepared than were students twenty years ago, and . . . training in languages at the undergraduate level shows a similar improvement."[23]

The *1980 Report* offered a much bleaker view of the state of foreign language instruction in the schools. Citing the President's Commission on Foreign Languages and International Studies, which had found that in 1979 only 15 percent of all high school students were studying a foreign language (compared to 24 percent in 1965), the authors of the *1980 Report* could readily "share the Commission's concern about low enrollments, and . . . support its recommendation that colleges 'reinvigorate language teaching in the schools' by raising the standards of their own requirements for admission."[24] They were "profoundly alarmed by what [they had] found: a serious deterioration in this country's language and research capacity."[25]

The *1980 Report* was but one of many voices expressing dismay at the decline of foreign language studies. Representative Paul Simon of Illinois, who has devoted much attention to this problem, noted in 1976 that only 4 percent of America's public high school students were taking more than two years of language studies.[26] In 1980 Simon and two congressional colleagues introduced a House resolution expressing the "sense of the Congress" that there is a need to strengthen course offerings and requirements in foreign languages and international studies, but the resolution never made it to the House floor. A bill introduced by Simon, the Foreign Language Assistance Act, suffered the same fate.

The consequences of this neglect may be serious. According to the deputy director of the Central Intelligence Agency, the nation's intelligence apparatus has been severely affected by deepening shortages of personnel trained in foreign languages.[27] As another observer put it, "The national interest requires that a capacity to teach all these languages be maintained, even through times when it is not heavily drawn upon."[28] Some difficult foreign languages require many years of study before fluency is attained, and it is unlikely that students will have sufficient incentive to study them if their prospects for getting a job are poor. According to the National Council on Foreign Language and International Studies, "The

present employment market for U.S. foreign area specialists fails
to reflect long-term needs, and . . . we lack sufficient capacities
to carry out the fundamental and applied research that is essential
to the conduct of our international political, economic, and cultural
affairs."[29]

During the first twelve years of its existence, NEH did nothing
formally to encourage applications to improve the teaching of foreign languages, although members of the NEH staff point out that
in the early 1970s the Education Division encouraged applications
in this area. In the late 1970s, however, the Education Division
announced that it welcomed applications in foreign language studies, and in its 1980 *Guidelines* the Division's Elementary and Secondary Grants Program actively sought applications for "projects to
improve teachers' and students' knowledge of . . . foreign languages." In general, the projects NEH has supported in this area
fall into three broad categories: summer institutes attended by high
school and/or college teachers seeking to improve their teaching of
foreign languages; new curricular materials for language instruction,
often designed to teach a language within a broad cultural context;
and new methods for teaching languages, especially individualized
instruction.

Some of these projects have been notable. In 1979 the University
of Maryland at Baltimore received a grant of $50,000 to overhaul
and restructure its language program, and it now offers an omnibus
B.A. in modern languages instead of separate majors in French,
German, or Spanish. Students have the choice of specializing in one
language or two, or in literature studies. In addition, all language
majors are required to take two courses taught in the English Department: "The World of Language," an introduction to the concept
of language, and "Textual Analyses," which shows how theories
and techniques of analytical reading and interpretation can apply to
all kinds of texts. The department also offers a third course, "World
Language Communities," designed mainly for non-language majors; it examines the phenomenon of language within a broad historical, social, and political context. The assumption behind these
three courses is that they will whet the appetites of students, providing the incentive to study foreign languages. According to the
codirector of the project, enrollment in foreign language courses has
increased by 30 percent since the program began.[30]

A three-year project at Ohio State University, funded beginning in 1977 by a grant of more than $800,000 from NEH, has also resulted in increased enrollments in foreign language courses, in this case by developing individual programs that students take in lieu of regular classroom instruction. According to the project directors, "teacher-assisted, mastery-based, self-paced instruction" is especially attractive to students who cannot enroll in regular classroom sections because of scheduling conflicts. It is also attractive to those who learn languages more slowly or more rapidly than most students. Using tapes and written materials, students study at home or in "learning centers" established by each of six departments in which a language can currently be studied in this manner. A teacher is always available to advise the student, who moves on to the next stage of study only when he or she has mastered the preceding one. The project directors, who claim that individualized attention is no more expensive than classroom instruction, believe it "can help considerably in increasing enrollments in foreign languages in this country." But they admit that the rate of attrition in such programs is high, and suspect that "lack of self-discipline is a major reason" why some students do not carry through with their intentions to learn a language.[31]

Yet another project supported by NEH focuses less on teaching a given language than on promoting interest in it. In 1978 the State University College of Potsdam, New York, was awarded a grant of $236,000 to develop a multimedia program designed to introduce elementary school children to the study of French. Thirty half-hour video shows offer a curriculum of some 250 French words, a small number of grammatical facts, a partial description of French phonology, and approximately a hundred facts and concepts about French history and culture. According to one expert who has evaluated this project, the likelihood that the children involved in the program will eventually elect to study French or another foreign language is "believed to have increased."[32]

NEH, then, has supported a number of projects designed to increase enrollments in foreign languages courses, but still enrollments have declined. Some observers have argued that the most important reason by far for the decline was the abolition of the language requirement for admission to college and/or for graduation. According to Representative Simon, "the United States continues to be the only country where you can graduate from college without having had one year of a foreign language prior to and during the university years."[33] Agreeing with the recommendations of the president's commission, which called late in 1979 for the reinstatement of foreign language requirements by high schools and colleges, a *Washington Post* editorial claimed: "Make a foreign language required for admission to college, and much else—not everything—follows." The single best way to promote the study of foreign languages, the editorial continued, "is to make it a college-entry requirement."[34]

If abolishing the foreign language requirement has been the most important factor in the decline of foreign language studies, then NEH cannot be said to have abetted that decline. In truth, NEH has had little effect one way or the other on the state of foreign language studies in the country's schools and colleges. But reinstituting the requirement, as the *Post* editorial suggested, will not necessarily cause foreign language studies to flourish. If required courses are poorly taught, then students will have little incentive either to learn a foreign language well or to major in this area. Richard Brod, the director of foreign language programs for the MLA, has argued that reinstating foreign language requirements is *not* a sensible policy for most colleges. "An artificial reason to take a foreign language course," he points out, "is not the best way to increase enrollments."[35] Other observers have held that requirements will do nothing to stimulate language teaching, and may actually hinder it by crowding classrooms with students who are uninterested in foreign language study.

The controversy surrounding the question of foreign language requirements illustrates the great difficulties encountered by NEH in its attempt to influence the course of American education. Even when NEH actively supports projects geared to the improvement of foreign language teaching, its efforts cannot mitigate the major factor affecting enrollment in foreign language courses. This factor is the importance that educators, parents, and scholars attach to the learning of a foreign language, and attitudes on this subject have been anything but static. In the late 1960s and early 1970s the foreign language requirement was generally regarded as an unnecessary burden upon students. Yet by the late 1970s, as we have already observed, the climate of educational opinion had changed, and many educators and scholars had come to a very different conclusion. "The era of educational parochialism appears to be drawing to an end," the education editor of the *New York Times* proclaimed in 1981. "Foreign languages and courses dealing with other cultures are making a modest comeback at all educational levels."[36] Also in 1981 the *Chronicle of Higher Education* noted that "for the first time in almost a decade foreign language teachers are optimistic about the future of their profession."[37] In the past few years more than seventy colleges and universities have reinstated foreign language requirements. But it seems unlikely that there will be a dramatic increase in the teaching of foreign languages at the elementary level, since most schools still do not offer languages to students under twelve. Moreover, in the past few years fifty-two colleges have dropped their courses in Russian, Chinese, and Japanese.

The modest increase in enrollment in foreign language courses, then, has less to do with NEH's efforts than with a change in the climate of educational opinion. During the 1960s, as *Newsweek* observed, "many schools—including such pace-setting institutions as Stanford and Yale—dropped language requirements and students opted for easier elective courses."[38] Their subsequent change of heart was abetted by the President's Commission on Foreign Languages and International Studies, but the commission would never have been formed in the first place if a number of educators, scholars, and government officials had not already come to the conclusion that the decline in the study of foreign languages was indeed a problem. It is hard to say how much NEH might have done to influence opinion in this area, but it is unlikely that the agency did very much. It relies heavily on the opinions of scholars in the humanities, and during the first decade of NEH's existence scholars did not generally believe that falling enrollments in foreign language courses were a problem.

EXPOSITORY WRITING

If many educators once believed it was not of paramount importance that students learn foreign languages, none ever said that students should neglect to learn how to write well in English. In the *1964 Report*, the MLA professed great concern about the state of writing in the nation's schools and colleges, noting gloomily that "in spite of the fact that 'English' is supposedly the one subject required in every grade of the lower schools as well as in a majority of colleges, we can report no such satisfaction in the improvement of the teaching of English as we feel in that of foreign languages." According to the MLA, "a majority of college students do not speak, write, or read their own language well." Yet after this public recognition of the problem, the MLA appeared to dismiss it, or rather to relegate it to the schools. "Our committee," the report admitted, "has no panacea to offer," adding that "whatever the causes, correction must come at the lower levels."[39]

Apparently the situation did not improve during the following fifteen years, for by the end of the 1970s most observers had come to the conclusion that, by and large, high school and college students were poorer writers than they had been in the 1960s. According to the authors of *Empty Pages: A Search for Writing Competence in School and Society* (1979), "We are all in some sort of trouble . . . over the teaching and learning of writing."[40] But some observers thought the cries of alarm were excessive, for teachers had always complained about the quality of their students' writing. It was misleading, these observers felt, to speak generally about a decline in writing; rather, it was the average college student's ability to write that had declined because the average student of the 1970s was significantly different from his counterpart of the 1960s. As one observer put it: "More and more students were being drawn from groups that a short time ago would never have even completed high school. And this trend has been exacerbated . . . as budget cutbacks and a declining birthrate have forced once selective colleges to dip lower and lower into the pool of applicants."[41]

Those who disagree point out that, in some cases, even students admitted to highly selective colleges are poor writers; the ability to write well, they say, has declined across all levels of intellectual ability. But these disagreements pale in significance in the face of the fact that by the mid-1970s virtually all educators had come to realize that most students, for whatever reason, were poor writers. And the *1980 Report*, unlike the *1964 Report*, devoted a good deal of attention to the teaching of expository writing.

During the first ten years of its existence, NEH discouraged applications dealing with the problem of writing, lest it appear to tread on the toes of the Department of Education, whose Office of School

Improvement supports projects to improve the teaching of basic skills. The agency is still uneasy about supporting projects focusing on the teaching of basic skills, but since the mid-1970s NEH has encouraged applications centering on the teaching of writing. In its *Eleventh Annual Report* the agency announced that "the Endowment's concern for the improvement of writing skills among college and high school students resulted in three grants during fiscal 1976."[42]

NEH decided to support writing-improvement projects not only because educators were complaining about the "writing crisis" but also because the teaching of writing was on the verge of becoming a legitimate specialty within the discipline of English. When the MLA suggested in the *1964 Report* that poor writing could be corrected only in the schools, it clearly implied that writing is not the concern of scholars in the humanities, that it is a basic skill that should be acquired before one becomes a serious student of the humanities. But by the mid-1970s many scholars had come to regard the teaching of writing as their responsibility, as a problem that should not be left to educators. A subtle change in the climate of educational opinion had transpired: the teaching of writing had become academically respectable. Indeed, many scholars who had heretofore devoted all their attention to writing literary criticism began to write about the teaching of writing. As a result, NEH began to receive many applications for the funding of writing-improvement projects, and in 1979 it expended $2.4 million on such projects.

In 1980 Chairman Duffey reported to Congress that expository writing was the one field in which NEH-supported projects had truly had a "nationally significant impact."[43] He was probably correct. He was also, in all likelihood, correct in singling out the National Writing Project (formerly the Bay Area Writing Project), to which NEH had awarded grants totaling approximately $1.7 million, as the most important NEH-supported project in the field of writing. Launched in 1974 but not awarded its first NEH grant until 1976, the National Writing Project has won high praise. "In conception, design, and execution," claim the authors of *Empty Pages*, "the project has set an example of what can and must be done if teachers are to become effective and self-assured in the teaching of writing."[44]

The National Writing Project is based on two elegantly simple assumptions: that students cannot learn to write well unless they are taught by teachers who themselves write well and often, and that students learn to write well by writing regularly. The project attacks a central weakness of the teaching of writing: the subject has historically been taught by scholars trained in the study of literature who resent having to teach writing and are bored by it. These teachers often feel uneasy and apprehensive about teaching written expression because they themselves do so little writing. Regarding this kind of teaching as an imposition, many have also neglected to assign sufficient written work. According to some reports, many students, owing to simple neglect on the part of teachers, have been assigned no more than three papers in three years of high school. A University of California report concludes that "for the majority of students, the problem lies not in a lack of natural ability or intelligence, but simply in the nature of previous instruction"[45]—or the lack of it. By 1983 the National Writing Project had trained more than 41,000 teacher consultants to work with other teachers to improve their teaching of writing. Several studies have shown that students taught by teachers who have undergone this training write better than other students.

In recent years NEH has funded two other large-scale projects whose common goal is the improvement of the teaching of writing. One, at the University of Iowa, is a six-month course for directors of freshman English programs from colleges throughout the nation. The participants not only study writing but also write papers themselves, and are subjected to constant criticism. At Beaver College the emphasis is on "writing across the curriculum," with faculty members in all disciplines involved in the project. Students practice writing in history, psychology, even mathematics, the essential point being that good writing should not be regarded only as the concern of the English department.

There is no doubt that even if NEH had not funded these and other projects the teaching of writing would have improved in the United States, for the climate of educational opinion was conducive to such improvement. As A. Graham Down, the executive director of the Council for Basic Education, has observed, the popularity of *Empty Pages* "indicates the near-universal recognition that writing improvement should be a supreme concern of educators at all levels."[46] *Time* agreed, noting in 1980 that a "wave of writing reform is sweeping through schools, colleges and businesses all over the U.S."[47] While NEH was not the instigator of this phenomenon, its support for several well-designed, large-scale projects no doubt hastened the change in educational opinion.

HISTORY

The *1964 Report* revealed that the teaching of history in the schools was suffering from a number of disabilities: "History tries to cover too much and becomes superficial; it is handicapped by duplication from one year to the next, and it is taught with too little emphasis on understanding and too much upon regurgitation of facts."[48] Among the recommendations of the American Historical Association was one that urged historians to "explore, describe, and teach the histories of the non-Western peoples."[49] The most striking feature of this report, however, was the confidence it exuded about the state of history in the schools and colleges. History, it said, "has become one of the central disciplines and indispensable experiences of liberal education."[50]

Fifteen years later, history—according to the *1980 Report*—had become quite dispensable: it was definitely losing out to social studies. This most recent report warned: "Courses in the social sciences should not supplant the study of geography and history. No young person should be expected to understand the complex conceptual models used in the social sciences without first learning a solid base of factual knowledge and critical skills through the study of history."[51] Some observers believe that "history classes [in the schools] are becoming a thing of the past."[52] The number of B.A.s conferred in history decreased from 37,381 in 1973-74 to 23,145 in 1977-78. Just as many educators had considered the study of foreign languages irrelevant in the late 1960s, in the early 1970s many regarded the study of history as irrelevant for certain students. "If you're a thinker, history is good for you," an educator who oversees the history and social studies program of a state school system said. "If you're going to go out and operate a drill press, then you don't need history."[53]

It is difficult to assess just how commonplace such an attitude was—and is—among educators. During the past fifteen years, the field of history has not been subject to the dramatic changes in educational opinion that have buffeted the fields of foreign languages and expository writing. But a distinct change in outlook did take place in the early 1970s, when many educators and some historians began to argue that social history, especially when it centers on the history of a local community or region, would revitalize the teaching of the discipline in the nation's schools and colleges. According to one educator, students are simply "turned off by traditional history," by which is meant political and intellectual history.[54] The *1980 Report* implied as much when it noted that "a promising recent development is the use of local historical resources in classes."[55]

The growth of courses in social history has been much abetted by NEH, which chose in the late 1970s to encourage applications in this area. In 1979 and 1980 social history grants represented approximately 75 percent of the awards made by the Education Division. To mention only a few of the largest: in 1979 the Newberry Library received $384,000 to run fifteen regional workshops and three summer institutes on the teaching of social history, and Carnegie-Mellon University won $282,000 to develop a secondary school social history curriculum. In the following year the Chicago Metro History Fair was awarded $129,000 to design, implement, and disseminate a "comprehensive interdisciplinary humanities unit introducing secondary students in Chicago public schools to the study of neighborhood history," and Greenfield Community College in Massachusetts was granted $261,000 to "create a new curriculum centering around the history and culture of the [local] area."[56]

The "Mid-South Humanities Project," an undertaking in community history to which NEH awarded $159,000 in 1980, was described in *Humanities* as an effort "designed to help classroom teachers show their students how to make their own regional heritage and history come alive." The project was alleged to have "sparked the study of history . . . in schools throughout the area."[57] But there is no evidence that those who take courses in local or community history gain the incentive to enroll in more traditional history courses, especially those with wider focuses. Robert Darnton, a professor of history at Princeton University, notes that the rise of social history has made it possible for students majoring in history to "know something about the rise of the black ghetto in Detroit and nothing about the decline of the Roman Empire."[58] In *The Past Before Us*, Michael Kammen applauds the recent burgeoning of interest in state, local, and family history, yet at the same time he is disturbed that "this reawakening of popular interest in the past, from all indications, has failed to dissipate the woeful ignorance on the part of most Americans about the basic narrative structure of their national history."[59] Some historians believe that the rise of social history may have contributed to this "woeful ignorance." According to one, social history leaves students with "an even narrower historical consciousness than that provided by the widely criticized political history of yesteryear."[60]

Social history is a loose term, a mansion containing many rooms, and it would be a mistake to argue that most social historians are hostile to political and intellectual history. It would be equally mistaken to allege that NEH has played a major role in the recent rise of social history. But there was no obvious need for NEH to encourage applications in this area, as there was for it to become involved in reforms in the teaching of expository writing. The study of history, like the study of foreign languages, was suffering the effects of a loss of faith on the part of educators (and even some historians) in the importance of historical knowledge. It was this loss of faith that led to the rise of social studies in the schools and to the abolition in many colleges of required courses in history. It led as well to a call for more relevant history—that is, for history about ordinary people rather than elites. NEH did nothing to instigate this change of outlook but, in effect, blessed it.

This brief survey of the efforts of NEH in three areas of the curriculum leaves us with the impression that the agency tends to amplify current educational concerns. NEH responded in the mid-1960s, when educators and scholars feared that the curriculum was rigid and inflexible, again in the late 1960s and early 1970s, when they were concerned that it did not sufficiently address contemporary issues, and yet again in the late 1970s and early 1980s, when they were worried that it was unstructured and neglected basic skills. As the *1980 Report* correctly observed, "The emphases of the Division of Education Programs have varied over the years, seemingly in step with the changing concerns of educators and the public."[61]

NEH may indeed amplify current educational concerns, but what happens in a particular school system depends less on the climate of national opinion than on prevailing attitudes in that system, or even in a particular school. The most effective schools, according to David Savage, have certain distinctive characteristics not, apparently, influenced by national educational opinion. Chief among them is a good principal, an "instructional leader" who cares about the academic program. Effective schools also tend to be "orderly without being rigid" and to focus on the teaching of basic skills.[62] Finally, in these schools the progress of students is frequently assessed. "The common denominator of successful schools, whether they are independent or public, inner-city or suburban," writes another observer, "is unconditional insistence upon high standards— in the teachers they hire, in the curricula they choose, and in the students they educate, slow and fast learners alike."[63] NEH can award grants intended to improve the teaching of particular subjects, but it cannot persuade individual school boards to hire "instructional leaders" or maintain "high standards."

It was not until William Bennett became chairman in 1982 that NEH began to stress the importance of improving the teaching of the humanities. Within a year the Education Division, having completely revamped its categories of support, issued a whole new set of guidelines. Moreover, Bennett began to speak out on educational matters in a forceful manner, something no previous NEH chairman had done. He charged that humanities courses in colleges and schools had degenerated into "a jumble of indiscriminate offerings" with "no rationale and no guidance or coherence for the mind or imagination." Taking a position closer to that of Matthew Arnold than to that of Robert Coles, he declared that "humanities education is no longer an introduction to the best [that is] thought and known."[64] He was not, however, in favor of a static curriculum, believing it the "responsibility of every generation of scholars and teachers not only to maintain the tradition of the humanities, but to extend and refine this tradition through new ideas and works."[65]

Was Bennett accurate in his description of the sorry state of the humanities in the nation's colleges and schools? After all, scholars and educators had already begun to wave the flag of tradition, and many colleges were trying to reinstitute core curricula. As Diane Ravitch, a professor of history and education at Columbia Teachers College, noted, "Since the mid-1970s the 'good school' has been eliminating frivolous courses, reinstating curricular requirements, and restoring academic standards."[66] Moreover, did Bennett accept

Arnold's view of the humanities uncritically—unjustifiably assigning humane studies an exalted position? It was one thing to say, as Bennett did, that the purpose of a humanistic education is to "enlarge the mind," but it was quite another to claim that the purpose of a humanistic education is to "save the soul" by providing not only "intellectual refinement" but also "spiritual elevation."[67]

Bennett's particular understanding of the humanities is probably less important than the specific changes he brought about in the Education Division, changes that reveal a shift in emphasis from course development to faculty development. By refraining from encouraging the development of new courses, NEH may be boosting the morale of educators who are worried about the fragmentation of the curriculum; and by encouraging various schemes of faculty development it may be raising faculty morale in general. According to A. Bartlett Giamatti, the president of Yale University, the quality and well-being of the faculty are "the most important issues facing us in education for the next difficult years."[68] Especially at the college level, the next decade or two may be difficult because decreasing enrollments and the specter of retrenchment may sap the morale of many teachers. Moreover, the general immobility of the profession, with most teachers frozen in their current positions, may lead to weariness and stagnation on the part of many college teachers.

A number of scholars and educators have come to the conclusion that one of the most effective ways of improving the teaching of the humanities is teachers' attendance at summer institutes. Such programs help teachers to overcome intellectual stagnation and to renew their interest in the subjects they teach. As the *1980 Report* noted, these institutes "may have more than an immediate effect on teaching performance. They can inspire teachers for the rest of their careers."[69] Under Bennett's chairmanship, NEH has increased its funding for summer institutes, especially for those that enable teachers to gain greater understanding of the subjects they teach.

NEH under Bennett has been especially concerned about the teaching of the humanities in secondary schools. It has given a grant of $800,000 to the Council for Basic Education to enable it to award $3,000 fellowships to ninety-nine high school teachers in order to conduct independent studies in the humanities during the summer. And it has established a new program, Summer Seminars for Secondary School Teachers, to give junior high school and high school teachers the opportunity to study humanistic texts in a collegial environment with a distinguished master teacher. But NEH's effort to improve secondary school teaching may be hampered by the generally poor quality of secondary school teachers. The *Washington Post* reported in 1979 that "the academic quality of the nation's young teachers is taking a nosedive as a shortage of jobs causes capable students to shun courses in education and look elsewhere."[70] This "education brain-drain," as one observer labeled it, has been most acutely felt in the secondary schools. The *1980 Report* lamented that "students in the field of education are typically among the least academically proficient undergraduates,"[71] an assessment supported by statistics. In a survey taken in 1976, college seniors with majors in education ranked fourteenth out of sixteen fields in both verbal and math SAT scores. And J. Myron Atkin has pointed out that in 1981 the average combined SAT score for high school seniors intending to prepare for teaching was 392, as opposed to 505 for future English majors.[72]

The authors of a recent study supported by the National Institute of Education believe that the brain drain is by no means only the result of a shortage of jobs in secondary education. They argue that "the relative position of teaching in the status structure of American occupations has declined over the past 30 years, so that its status as a white collar job is even more marginal than in the past."[73] Teaching, they claim, no longer attracts the highly able women and minority youths who once considered it a preferred profession. The *1980 Report* agrees that "the low status of the teaching profession is a national disgrace and an obstacle to improving education in the schools."[74] Also in agreement is Ernest Boyer, the president of the Carnegie Fund for the Advancement of Learning, who recently observed that "the quality of education in this nation can rise no higher than the quality of teachers. If public support continues to decline, and if teaching standards continue to go down, the intellectual and economic future of this nation will be threatened."[75]

NEH, it would seem, can do little to improve the status of secondary school teachers except perhaps to draw attention to the problem by means of conferences and speeches by NEH staff. It might force particular attention on the discrepancy between the nation's demand for excellence in education and its general unwillingness to pay secondary school teachers salaries that are competitive with others in the human-services field. But the agency can do nothing about the passing of the baby-boom generation, which has already resulted in dwindling enrollments and which in the next decade will cause the number of students at colleges and universities to drop an estimated 10 to 15 percent.[76] And it cannot directly help colleges facing low enrollments, making it difficult for them to maintain high standards, resist grade inflation, impose requirements for admission or graduation, and eliminate trivia from the curriculum.[77] Sadly, if colleges lower their requirements, high schools will undoubtedly follow suit.

Despite the status of secondary school teachers and the gloomy financial situation of many colleges and universities, NEH can have some effect, albeit limited, on certain aspects of humanities education. As we have seen, its grants have made a difference in some areas, especially expository writing. But how much money is necessary in order for NEH to have a favorable impact? The *1980 Report* recommended doubling NEH's budget for elementary and secondary education, yet some observers believe that, paradoxically, an abundance of funds would be harmful rather than beneficial. Ralph W. Tyler has argued that "during times of material affluence we become engrossed in pursuing dollars; but when dollars are not available we seek, if we are wise, to raise the quality of education and attack some of the serious problems we face."[78] In other words, the availability of grant monies tends to be a distraction, inducing educators to become more preoccupied with finding ways to tap government funds than with improving the quality of education in their schools or districts.

In any case, those who argue that more federal funds will stem the decline in education neglect the obvious point that the decline in the teaching of both the sciences and the humanities had less to do with a lack of federal funds than with a lack of commitment to rigorous education on the part of educators and scholars. Commenting on the fact that the number of students who achieve high scores on college entrance examinations has fallen drastically since the early 1970s, Richard Berendzen, the president of American University, said: "There's been a diminution of rigor in the schools since the mid-1960s, and this seems to be one of the results."[79] And

Alexander Astin, a professor of education at UCLA, is convinced that "the schools are just less demanding than they used to be and [students] are lazy up and down the ability spectrum."[80]

What is needed now is not merely a higher level of funding but a more careful use of existing funds, for NEH has squandered much of its money for education on the development of new courses, new curricula, and new curricular materials. In the future it might profitably devote more of its efforts to seeking out and rewarding excellent teachers as well as excellent methods of teaching. NEH also should encourage the formulators of large-scale projects to seek private as well as NEH funds. Projects to improve the quality of teaching have rarely looked to the private sector for support, despite the fact that, according to the *Wall Street Journal*, "the troubles that have beset U.S. classrooms in recent years are increasingly felt in the nation's offices and factories."[81] To deal with growing numbers of semiliterate workers, many corporations are already providing instruction in writing and mathematics. A study of education in industry completed in 1976 found that 35 percent of some 800 companies provided instruction in subjects that "are really the responsibility of the schools."[82] To date, more than 200 corporations provide financial and personnel aid for the nation's public schools.[83] Scholars and educators alike should look more to business for support, for business can help fund efforts to improve local school systems.

If it is not clear that more federal funds are needed to improve the teaching of the humanities in the nation's schools, it is clear that more federal funds are needed to remedy a significant national problem: the lack of a cadre of scholars proficient in difficult languages (Russian, Chinese, Japanese, and Arabic, for example) and well versed in the culture and history of the countries where these languages are spoken. The private sector can help, in fact has already helped, to remedy this situation. The recent bequest by W. Averell Harriman of $10 million to Columbia University to expand its Russian Institute into the W. Averell Harriman Institute for the Advanced Study of the Soviet Union will add faculty members, attract gifted new students, and establish a computerized data bank on Soviet affairs open to scholars from around the world.[84] The institute will undoubtedly do much to foster Russian studies in the United States, but more such centers are needed for the study of other languages and cultures. The president's commission recommended federal support for centers of international training and research to train foreign area specialists, both scholars and teachers. Whether these centers, which would focus on major world regions and issues, are supported by NEH or another federal agency is a relatively unimportant question. That such centers are needed is clear.

Yet whatever support NEH gives for the teaching of foreign languages, writing, history, or other areas of the humanities, the agency can have little impact unless other federal agencies, state and local school boards, school principals, and teachers are determined to make schools better places in which to learn. In the spring of 1983 the weakness of American education became a national issue after three task forces published reports about the sorry state of learning in America. Calling for "deep and lasting change" in American education, the National Task Force on Education for Economic Growth argued that low expectations and mediocre performance in public schools threatened the United States' economic position in the world. The National Commission on Excellence in Education decried what it termed the "rising tide of mediocrity" in American public schools and called for longer school days and better pay for teachers. Finally, a task force sponsored by the Twentieth Century Fund called for a federally sponsored "master teachers program" that would provide the best teachers in every state with bonuses of up to $40,000 a year.[85]

The reports suddenly made education a hot political issue—one taken up with alacrity by President Reagan and most of the Democratic candidates for the presidency. Reagan called for merit pay for teachers, whereas Senator Ernest F. Hollings called for a federally financed $5,000-a-year pay raise for public school teachers. "If we want good teachers, we will have to pay for them," Hollings said. "It's as simple as that."[86] While acknowledging the need for better teachers, other observers said that American education had declined in part because of the fragmentation of American families. Pointing out that federal and state assistance for education had increased dramatically during the 1960s and 1970s, a period when educational quality was in decline, Victor Fuchs, an economist at Stanford, argued that the schools have had "to devote time and money to cope with the discipline and instructional problems" resulting from the rise of one-parent families in which the parent has little or no time to spend with the children. According to Fuchs, "There can be little doubt that the investments parents make in their children and the values they instill in them are major determinants of how the children will fare in school. The success of children of Asian background in U.S. public schools provides vivid testimony that study, hard work, respect for teachers and heavy parental involvement in the educational progress of children still pay off."[87]

Yet even Fuchs admitted that "we need to improve the schools and we need to support them adequately."[88] In 1983, Congress came to the conclusion that schools were not adequately supported. In March the House passed, by a heavily bipartisan vote of 348 to 54, a bill calling for a $425 million federal commitment in the coming fiscal year to improve education in mathematics, science, and foreign language instruction in the nation's schools. As of June 1983 no bill had passed the Senate, but more than fifteen proposals had been offered and it seemed likely that a measure sponsored by Senator Pell and Senator Robert T. Stafford, a Republican from Vermont, had the best chance for passage. It would provide $400 million in federal aid to schools. Although the White House hinted that the president might veto such costly legislation, there was a good chance that such a veto would be overridden.

Where does NEH stand in what promises to be a new federal effort to improve American education? During the remainder of the 1980s it is likely that the percentage of NEH's budget allotted to education will increase somewhat, but NEH will never provide major financial support for American education. Nevertheless, NEH can play a significant role in defining how education should be improved by supporting model projects that in different ways enable teachers to improve their teaching of the humanities.

8

Public Programs
in the Humanities

ON DECEMBER 8, 1982, the National Endowment for the Humanities achieved a first in its comparatively short history: a meeting with the president in the Oval Office of the White House to announce a number of grants. Although the meeting was very much a public event, the grants were not for public programs such as television series or museum exhibits. Rather, they were challenge grants to thirteen independent research libraries that together would collect more than $5 million if they could raise $15 million in private contributions. The New York Public Library alone was awarded $2 million, the largest challenge grant ever given by NEH to a single institution. Smaller amounts were awarded to such leading research libraries as the Folger Shakespeare Library in Washington; the Huntington Library in San Marino, California; and the Newberry Library in Chicago. The funds for these grants had originally been allocated to NEH's Division of Public Programs (the title of which was changed under William Bennett to the Division of General Programs) but they had never been expended in that division because, according to Bennett, there simply were not enough good applications on which to spend so large a sum.[1]

Whatever the reason for the reallocation of funds, the symbolism of the Oval Office announcement was clear: NEH's primary concern was no longer the general public but the scholarly community. If anyone had missed the point, Bennett stressed it in a subsequent interview. The challenge grants to research libraries, he said, signaled NEH's "interest, in a time of . . . budget reductions, in focusing on essential resources, [on] institutions that are the generators for some of the most important work in the humanities." More NEH money, he went on, was now going into research and "special initiative projects," such as the library grants, and less into public programs.[2] With this shift in emphasis, Bennett was following in Duffey's footsteps, for Duffey had also proposed cuts in NEH's support for public programs. Defending the budget he submitted to Congress, Duffey remarked in 1981 that he felt compelled to "protect the things that are going to have the hardest time getting any funding [from private sources]—the classification and preservation of archives, for instance."[3]

In the 1970s there had been rapid and substantial growth in public programs, from 16 percent of the NEH budget in 1970 to approximately 50 percent in 1980. But with the administration's threatened cutbacks, it was apparent that in the 1980s the trend would be reversed. Commenting on the proposed budget for 1983, an observer in *Humanities Report* noted: "Increased priority is given to those programs devoted to teaching and scholarship, while funding for most programs having the general public as their audience is shrinking. . . . Public Programs and Special Programs, long bedevilled by criticism and often seen as low priorities, take the largest cuts."[4] The only area of express benefit to the public that escaped cuts was State Programs, entitled by law to at least 20 percent of NEH's program funds.

Why the change in the agency's direction? For one thing, there had long been vague dissatisfaction with public programs on the grounds that the benefits derived from them did not justify their high costs. But to speak in such general terms about public programs does not provide a satisfactory answer since different public programs had enjoyed different rates of success. Instead, we must look closely at four broad areas of funding for public programs: grants to state humanities committees (which "regrant" these funds to support public programs in the humanities); grants to independent producers and to television and radio stations for the production of programs for the electronic media; grants to museums, historical organizations, and libraries for exhibits and discussion groups; and grants to a wide variety of other public organizations, especially national membership groups, such as the American Association of Retired Persons (AARP) and the League of Women Voters, to develop and present programs in the humanities. Until recently there were three NEH divisions involved in these areas: State Programs, Public Programs, and Special Programs. In 1982, however, NEH combined the latter two under the rubric of General Programs.

STATE PROGRAMS

The state humanities committees, originally organized in response to congressional insistence that NEH institute something similar to NEA's state arts council program, have engendered a great deal of controversy. The main point of contention has been the state committees' identity: should they be independent bodies or agencies of the states, like NEA's state arts councils? The NEA model has so far proven unsuccessful for NEH: in 1970 the agency awarded grants of $100,000 to state arts councils in Oklahoma and Maine to establish humanities subcommittees as part of their general programs, but both of the newly created subcommittees asked to be severed from their parent arts councils when it became obvious that the humanities programs were not flourishing under the auspices of arts councils. The ensuing controversy, which pitted both Berman and Duffey against Senator Pell, flared at NEH reauthorization hearings in 1975 and again in 1979. In each case the NEH chairman argued that state humanities committees should remain independent, while Pell preferred to see these committees become "full partner[s] in state government, [with] a status comparable to that of the state arts councils."[5]

According to NEH, independent state humanities committees rather than state agencies were established for several reasons:

Every state had a number of tax-supported and private agencies with a partial interest in the humanities, and nearly equal claims to be selected as the agency for an Endowment program in the state. . . . The existing groups, however, were designed to support only one or a few of the disciplines of the humanities, or were designed for more than one purpose. . . . A new organization was a way to give many of these groups a voice and at the same time address *all* of the humanities. In addition, a new organization could focus on the single task of increasing public understanding and appreciation of the humanities.[6]

In order to establish the new state committees, the NEH staff surveyed the landscape of the humanities in each state and drew up lists of one hundred or more people from each state who were in some way connected with the humanities. After consulting with many of these people about who would be best able to contribute to the creation of state humanities programs, NEH invited six consultants from each state to come to Washington for intensive discussions about the new program. Following this meeting, participants were expected to apply to NEH for planning grants and to begin the process of shaping programs for their states. Apart from these catalytic groups, NEH had no role in the selection of members for state committees, although the agency did stipulate that they should be composed in equal parts of people from three different groups: administrators of cultural and educational institutions, scholars in the humanities, and members of the general public. All committee members were to serve without pay.

Senator Pell has thought all along that the NEH staff played too great a role both in setting up and in guiding the state committees. At the 1975 reauthorization hearings, he described the formation of these committees as a "laying-on of hands" from Washington.[7] Four years later, when introducing the 1979 NEH reauthorization bill in Congress, he complained that "the only mechanisms of control and counsel are the [NEH] staff on the one hand and the volunteer citizens committees on the other. The membership of these committees has little formal provision for external, broad public influence."[8] According to Pell, the independence of the committees meant that they were not accountable to the citizens of their states and that they would probably never become, as he put it, either "accessible" or "visible." "It is my firm belief," he declared, "that under a true federal-state partnership system . . . the current programs will thrive as they become ever more visible and more accessible."[9]

Both NEH and the members of most state committees questioned Pell's prescription. NEH stressed the importance of having volunteer committees: "By engaging citizens who were united through a common sense of purpose and dedication to the humanities, the Endowment expected that significant public programs in the humanities could be accomplished without putting in place a costly delivery system."[10] According to Elspeth Rostow, dean of the Lyndon B. Johnson School of Public Affairs at the University of Texas, if Pell's plan were to prevail, NEH would "lose the reservoir of volunteers which show America still has a community sense."[11] A study prepared by the Texas Committee for the Humanities argued that the state committees' independence is the only guarantee of their neutrality, perhaps their greatest asset.[12] Pell's plan had its supporters, but a statement in the *1980 Report* probably reflected a consensus of opinion: "In our view the spontaneity and creative freedom from bureaucratic obstruction demonstrated by many State Committees more than outweigh any possible advantages of integrating them with the political system of the state."[13]

Faced with widespread opposition, Pell relented somewhat, eventually supporting compromise legislation that changed the makeup of the state committees without destroying their independence. This legislation, passed in 1976, required committees to spell out their operating procedures, especially in such matters as the length of service of committee members and the rotation of officers. It also mandated the establishment by each committee of "a membership policy which is designed to assure broad public representation." State governors were authorized to appoint a minimum of two members; if a state awarded funds to its committee, the governor could, according to a graduated formula, appoint up to half the members. Legislation enacted in 1980 made even stronger the connection between state governments and state humanities committees: a governor could appoint at least four members to his state's committee and was even empowered to make the committee a state agency if the state "provided either 50 percent of its basic operating grant from NEH ($200,000) or 25 percent of the total support received from NEH, whichever is greater."[14] To date, no state has chosen to turn its humanities committee into an agency of state government; three states (Virginia, Minnesota, and Alaska) have appropriated some funds for their committees but have shown no interest in making them into state agencies.

What should be made of this often tedious quarrel? According to Pell, the state committees, insulated from the political process, had become coteries of nepotism that awarded grants and committee appointments to friends. He also argued that the committees were too closely associated with academe. If the state committees became more like state arts councils, he believed, they would be more likely to have a beneficial influence. Pell was unable to marshal concrete evidence to show that the state committees were exclusive coteries, but it is true that they were closely associated with the academy, since many of those who are well versed in humanistic disciplines are college or university professors. NEH held out against Pell's scheme because it believed, as did most people associated with the program, that the transformation of the committees into state agencies would lower the quality of state programs. They voiced the fear that political pressures would henceforth play a greater role in the awarding of grants, a fear Pell dismissed as self-serving.

However one views the question of the relationship between humanities committees and their respective states—a question that dominated the reauthorization hearings of both 1975 and 1979—it is a less important question than Pell made it out to be. A much more important question is what state committees should do. When NEH began to form the committees in the early 1970s, it believed that they could build large audiences for public programs in the humanities only if they concentrated on issues of public policy, an argument put most forcefully by John Barcroft, an NEH official considered to be the major architect of the state programs. "The focus on genuine public policy issues," Barcroft asserted in 1973, "is crucial. . . . It is what gives the program its moral urgency; and without it the program is in danger of becoming an interesting anomaly and no more."[15]

Many scholars in the humanities applauded NEH's efforts to encourage scholars to participate in public programs focusing on questions of public policy. According to the late Charles Frankel: "Nothing has happened of greater importance in the history of American humanistic scholarship than the invitation of the government to scholars to think in a more public fashion, and to think and teach with the presence of their fellow citizens in mind." Frankel, a professor of philosophy at Columbia University and the first head of the National Humanities Center, urged NEH to "lay down a challenge" to scholars and "put [its] capacities for vision, lucidity, and dispassionate civic commitment to the test."[16] Other scholars, while endorsing the general idea of state programs, objected to the public policy focus. In 1978, for example, William Bennett, then executive director of the National Humanities Center, accused the national meeting of state committees of sponsoring "boring" work. "You force humanists to talk about things they know nothing about," he said. "It doesn't show humanists at their best."[17] In 1981 Robert Hollander, a professor of literature at Princeton and a former member of the National Council, was even more blunt than Bennett had been. According to Hollander, "Weak thinking in Washington and confused acquiescence around the country have caused the understandable results—watered down humanistic programs which are ill-disguised ventures into political and social enthusiasms and which more often stir up feelings than produce thought."[18]

The remarks of both Bennett and Hollander may seem academic, since in 1976 Congress had mandated that the state committees pursue all of the options open to NEH—in short, to become, if they so desired, mini-NEHs. All states have since broadened their areas of support, but far more money has been given to public programs than to research. Some states fund research that is disseminated in public lectures, discussion programs, or publications, and some also fund humanist-in-residence projects, placing scholars, especially philosophers, in institutional settings (departments of mental health, state prisons, hospitals, etc.) to help illuminate the problems facing those who work in such institutions. But the biggest beneficiary of the broadened focus of the state committees has been state and local history projects. At least half the state programs have established funding categories for projects to interpret local history, culture, or art.[19]

Even though the state committees no longer concentrate exclusively on issues of public policy, they still award a significant number of grants to policy projects. Were Bennett and Hollander right in questioning the appropriateness of scholarly involvement in questions of public policy? There is no doubt that the state humanities committees were unduly restricted by the requirement that they focus only on this area, but the notion that today's scholars, especially historians and philosophers, are incapable of discussing public policy would have puzzled a host of thinkers (from Dante to the authors of *The Federalist*) who have been called civic humanists precisely because they believed that scholarship could help to clarify issues of public policy.

The role scholars play in public policy discussions is critical. As Richard Wasserstrom, a professor of philosophy at UCLA, has put it, scholarly participation in this area can help us to "understand more clearly what the questions are and how to go about thinking of them."[20] The scholarly contribution is especially significant because a scholar's depth of knowledge often goes far beyond that of the nonscholar. James Madison and Alexander Hamilton, for example, were monumentally important figures in the drawing up of the American Constitution largely because they had read deeply on the theory of republican government as well as on the history of ancient and modern republics. Scholars, of course, are also citizens, and they may hold strong views on particular questions of public policy, but their participation in public-policy projects should stem from their knowledge and analytical skills rather than from their private views.

It is impossible to assess whether or not scholars who participate in public programs envision their role in this way. The defense of the humanities put forward in the *1964 Report* and the *1980 Report* implies that scholars somehow inculcate humanistic "values," representing the world of the spirit as opposed to the world of commerce, consumerism, or "materialism." The *1980 Report*, for example, asks, "Shall we interpret the phrases *quality of life* and *leisure time* in a material or a spiritual sense?"[21] If most scholars assume that in discussions of public policy they are obliged to take the "spiritual" side while businessmen and engineers emphasize the "material," this would mean that state programs have succeeded only in reinforcing intellectual complacency and moral smugness among scholars in the humanities.

Charles Frankel believed that the greatest aim of state programs, rather than getting more Americans to think about humanistic "values," should be to encourage scholars to question their own views, and by so doing to revitalize the humanities. "I don't think the National Endowment for the Humanities is trying to save America by bringing the humanities to bear on public issues," Frankel observed, ". . . but it might do something to revive the humanities."[22] Certainly some scholars have benefited from participation in state humanities projects, and some have even changed the direction of their scholarly work—in particular, philosophers who have become more interested in the way in which their discipline can help to illuminate issues of public policy. But we cannot say that the humanities have been "revitalized" because of state programs in particular or public programs in general. In all likelihood NEH's State Programs Division has had only a minimal effect on the state of the humanities.

Perhaps Frankel in calling for "revitalization" was asking too much of the State Programs Division. Just how effective has the division been in reaching the public with programs in the humanities? In 1973 John Barcroft expressed the hope that by 1976 the humanities would have "so fully infused [each state program] that everyone in the United States will see this . . . as manifestly a program in the humanities."[23] It is evident that such expectations have not been met, but its shortcomings do not mean that the State Programs Division is a failure. Reporting to Congress in 1980, Duffey predicted that in the following year state committees would support approximately 3,000 projects that should reach as many as twenty-nine million people.[24] These figures, which are "soft" since they are based in part on estimates of television audiences, are nevertheless impressive. According to a number of observers, state programs have had a significant impact, especially in such rural states as Vermont, South Dakota, and Montana, perhaps because in small, rural communities meetings on controversial issues of public policy are better attended, in proportion to population, than similar meetings in urban areas.

Despite their often positive impact, evaluating state programs fairly is difficult; the state committees' "awesome task" has been undertaken with varying degrees of success.[25] State committees evaluate projects, or at least solicit evaluations from project directors as well as from independent observers. State committees also collect statistics on the number of people who benefit from projects. But even the executive directors of state committees have a hard time generalizing about the quality of the programs in their states, since they can personally evaluate only a relatively small percentage of the projects they fund. They do, of course, know something about the impact of certain projects, but it is sometimes difficult for them to assess whether or not a given project is well grounded in the humanities. According to Ronald Florence, the former director of the New York Council for the Humanities, most projects are "either real humanities programs nobody goes to, or they're popular programs that have nothing to do with the humanities."[26]

One way of assessing the programs of different states—albeit an indirect one—is to count the number of well-known scholars in the humanities who serve on various committees, scholars who would presumably refuse to be associated with state programs not strongly grounded in the humanities. But assessing committees on the basis of this criterion is risky, for a committee without distinguished scholarly representation but made up of solid academic humanists who take a strong interest in its programs might well be more effective than a committee composed of highly visible scholars whose interest is slight.

In 1980 the Federation of Public Programs in the Humanities commissioned Charles C. Cole, Jr., executive director of the Ohio Program in the Humanities, to do a study of innovative public humanities programs—those "in which effective instructional methods and informal formats were used or in which there was extensive dialogue between humanities scholars and the general public."[27] After reviewing 125 project proposals recommended by executive directors of state committees, as well as descriptions and evaluation reports from 31 states, and attending 15 humanities programs, Cole selected 91 humanities projects funded by state committees that were "distinguished for their innovative formats or their success in generating strong audience participation."[28] The list, however, is not particularly revealing. For one thing, the descriptions are too brief to be meaningful, and for another, many of the projects do not seem to fulfill Cole's main criteria; they lacked "extensive dialogue" between humanities scholars and the public or suffered from poor audience participation. But we also need to question Cole's criteria; programs that win high audience participation are not necessarily the most strongly humanistic.

It is not easy to evaluate any of NEH's programs, but it is fair to say that when NEH gives a research fellowship to a scholar or a challenge grant to a research library it is directly supporting the humanities. The State Programs Division demands careful scrutiny because many of the projects the state committees have supported seem only marginally related to the humanities. Yet owing to the provisions of the reauthorizing legislation of 1976, NEH is locked into spending 20 percent of its funds on state programs. By spelling out this level of support, Congress not only gave the committees its blessing, it also made it exceedingly difficult for NEH to judge the State Programs Division on its own merits.

In 1979 an observer wrote that "even the harshest critics have words of praise for the hard work and earnest intentions of the [state] committees."[29] In one respect, State Programs has been a success: an impressive number of people have been willing to serve on state committees in positions that are both time-consuming and un-remunerative. Presumably they are willing to do so because they believe the state programs are worth supporting, or at least have the potential to be effective. Yet William Havard, a professor of polit-ical theory at Vanderbilt University who has served on state com-mittees, wonders whether this volunteer effort has produced much in the way of results: "I have been most impressed by the spon-taneity and enthusiasm with which so many volunteers have re-sponded to NEH's efforts to develop these programs. But I have some strong reservations about the total effect of the programs rel-ative to the commitment of resources and energy that have been made to them . . . . Most of the programs have been short term, single shot efforts, with insufficient attention being paid to re-peating programs for different audiences or developing variations on, or extensions of, programs that were judged to be successful."[30]

During Duffey's incumbency NEH paid relatively little attention to the state committees, but Bennett, after his appointment as chair-man, decided to do something about what he believed was the poor quality of many state programs. He offered state committees re-wards for excellence—Chairman's Awards of $75,000 for exem-plary projects. According to *Humanities*, NEH's official newsletter, an exemplary project is one that "relies . . . on the tools and dis-ciplines that are at the heart of humanities study to carry out the mandate of state committees."[31] The awards, according to Bennett, "grew from a desire to identify certain areas of excellence and en-courage further development in them."[32] He also served notice on the state committees that, if their proposals were poor in quality— programs, that is, in which the humanities were weakly repre-sented—their funding would be reduced. The Division of State Pro-grams has recently released a document entitled "Initiatives 1983," setting forth five areas of concentration: (1) clearer and stronger articulation by NEH of the intellectual purpose and standards of a program; (2) enforcement of standards and rewards for excellence; (3) modification of the regrant principle, allowing a state council to use a small percentage of its grant funds to conduct a single, coher-ent humanities project; (4) strengthened efforts at orientation and education of council members and staff; and (5) continuation of the special competition for the awards for excellence.[33]

It is too soon to say whether these guidelines will have an effect on the state committees, but Bennett's insistence upon playing an active role vis-à-vis the state committees has already stirred up resentment. Many states do not want NEH to be the arbiter of what constitutes good state programs. There is some justice to these complaints, since NEH has changed its mind about just what it wants the state committees to do; after first insisting that they focus on public policy, NEH later encouraged them to move away from this area. William Brennan, the executive director of the Florida Endowment for the Humanities, spoke for many executive directors when he questioned why state committees, which are required to submit biannual proposals that undergo peer review at NEH, should be reviewed by NEH at all. "Why do we use the word 'proposal,'" Brennan asked, "to refer to the 'reports' called for by Congress, as if the state-based endowments were not permanent programs?"[34] The process of peer review of the state committees' programs, he went on, is senseless: "Why do we presume that a group of ten or so presumably intelligent and almost certainly well-intentioned persons, perhaps half of whom have no prior experience with the state-based program, can meet one time . . . and make judgments of program performance and direction [on the basis of reading a single report]?"[35] The review process, Brennan added, consumes an inordinate amount of time—time that the administrators of state programs could use to better purpose.

Whether or not all executive directors would agree with Brennan's remarks, State Programs, beset by controversy, is NEH's most problematical program. Should individual state programs be reviewed by NEH every other year, as if they were not altogether permanent? Would state committees be more effective if they were state agencies? Should they pursue a wide variety of programming to the point of undertaking projects themselves rather than regranting their funds? And—the most difficult question of all—how can we determine whether the state programs are worth what they cost, whether, indeed, they are worth keeping in existence?

MEDIA PROJECTS

In its *Second Annual Report*, NEH spoke of "strengthening the capacities of television . . . to handle material of humanistic content."[36] In the early years of its existence, however, the agency supported few such projects, and it had no separate budget category for media proposals until 1972. The program grew so slowly, it seems, because few people involved in the media were interested in producing programs centering on the humanities. Finally, in the mid-1970s, NEH attempted to stimulate the growth of humanities programming by awarding planning grants, averaging $15,000, to public broadcasting organizations as well as to independent filmmakers and unaffiliated radio and television stations. These grants, under which humanist consultants were hired to discuss programming possibilities in the humanities, evidently paid off. Applications to NEH to develop humanities projects for radio and television increased dramatically, with the number of new grantees rising from 42 to 160 between 1976 and 1980. The NEH budget for Humanities Projects in Media rose from less than $1 million in 1972 to more than $9 million in 1980.

Since 1967 NEH has spent approximately $65 million on media projects. About half of this sum was awarded directly to public television and radio stations for production, and the rest to independent producers. Today NEH is the fourth-largest source of federal funding for public television, and NEH-supported projects have won some sixty-five awards.[37] Among the most widely praised NEH-sponsored programs was *American Short Story*, which adapted classic American stories into thirty-minute films for television and was the first series produced by American public television to be purchased by the BBC. *Odyssey*, a series of documentary films in which research done by anthropologists and archaeologists was used to explore a wide variety of cultures, has also been favorably received. Yet despite these and other successes, the NEH budget for media was reduced in the early 1980s by approximately 50 percent.

Although the cuts were actually made during the first year of Bennett's chairmanship, Duffey had earlier planned to make them. "Public television just costs too much,"[38] he said in 1981. Both he and Bennett believed the private sector was more likely to underwrite the costs of television series than of scholarly productions such as dictionaries or editions of the papers of distinguished Americans. NEH may also have decided to reduce its support for media projects because of the difficulty of setting up a review process for media proposals that would be both judicious and efficient. Writing about the film production of Henry James's *The Europeans*, funded by the British National Film Finance Corporation after having been rejected by NEH, a critic for the *New York Times* implied that NEH's bureaucratic procedures made it unlikely that meritorious proposals would be rewarded.[39] The *1980 Report* alluded to this problem when it admitted that NEH's procedures "can present bureaucratic, artistic, and financial problems that make production difficult at best."[40]

NEH's procedures, especially its recommendation that funding be sought in stages (first for scriptwriting, then for production), may be cumbersome, but it is difficult to see how they could be otherwise, given the necessity for federal agencies to be cautious in dispensing funds for expensive projects. The chief complaint, though, has been about NEH's requirement that scholars in the humanities be closely associated with media projects. According to one observer, "Many producers feel that having 'academic humanists' on their productions is the burden they bear in order to be funded."[41] To be sure, some projects require scholarly consultants—those, for example, centering on archaeology or the re-creation of particular historical periods—but it is far from clear why a filmmaker adapting a novel by Henry James for the screen needs a scholarly collaborator. By imposing such a requirement, NEH is suggesting that only those with advanced degrees in humanistic disciplines are capable, as an NEH brochure puts it, of ensuring that a given project "uses resources from the humanities in a way which adds depth to the subject."[42]

The requirement points to a greater weakness: NEH's preoccupation with "subjects and issues that are central to the humanities." In order to demonstrate that what it supports is different from what NEA supports, NEH has insisted that projects be strongly grounded in the humanities. But often it is not obvious whether a given project lies within the arts or the humanities. For example, in the early days of Humanities Projects in Media, the NEH staff wrangled over the question of whether the production of one of Shakespeare's plays was an arts or a humanities project, finally deciding that only if the production were introduced by a scholar in the humanities was it clearly within the purview of the humanities.

Although individuals involved in public television and radio complained about NEH's requirements and procedures, they relied upon the agency for support, and in 1982 voiced their strong disapproval of both the shift of funds in that year's budget from Media Projects to challenge grants for research libraries, and the 50 percent cut for Media Projects, which NEH had submitted to Congress for 1983. Larry Sapadin, the executive director of the Association for Independent Video and Film, called the shift of funds "a show of Bennett's contempt for media as an expression of the humanities,"[43] while Bruce Christensen, president of the National Association of Public Television Stations, lamented that one reason why the quality and quantity of grant applications to Media Projects had fallen off was because "effective interaction" between applicants and NEH "has been virtually eliminated."[44]

Both Duffey and Bennett were dissatisfied with Media Projects, partly because of the cost of programming and the controversies over review procedures and requirements. But the main reason both men decided to allocate fewer funds to Media Projects was their conviction that cultural programming—if not necessarily programming lying within "the humanities," narrowly defined—could (and would) be paid for by private sources such as the major corporations. Perhaps they had also read the reports of numerous commentators who held that the advent of cable television would make a self-supporting cultural network financially viable. Indeed, in the late 1970s and early 1980s four cable networks offering cultural programs came into being: ABC's ARTS, the Bravo network, CBS Cable, and RCA's Entertainment Channel.

By the spring of 1982, however, two of these networks had folded: CBS Cable after having lost $30 million, and RCA's Entertainment Channel after having lost $34 million. There was growing uncertainty that cultural programming could thrive without government support. Commenting on the demise of CBS Cable, John J. O'Connor, television critic for the *New York Times*, observed, "As CBS hastily retreats from the cultural programming arena, the need for devising effective means to fund the public system is more crucial than ever."[45] Many public television stations were in dire financial straits. In the fall of 1982, for example, the New York metropolitan area's major public television station (WNET) abruptly postponed a multimillion-dollar series and contemplated staff reduction in the face of a $6 million deficit.[46]

Despite these problems, some observers believed that the need for public support was not demonstrable. Everyone concerned agreed that, even though CBS's and RCA's ventures into cultural programming had failed, there was a growing audience for this kind of programming. "With each passing season," O'Connor noted, "the ratings have substantiated the fact that there is a receptive audience for quality programming."[47] Moreover, CBS Cable did reach five million homes. W.S. James, vice-president for video technology/programming at a leading advertising agency, spoke for many when he remarked, "There is a market for culture on cable."[48] CBS Cable had failed, James said, because of bad management: "They spent a lot of money and were unrealistic about it being profitable in its first year."[49] Others have agreed with James's assessment. CBS Cable spent lavishly to originate 60 percent of its own programming, compared with 25 percent for ABC's ARTS.[50] It may well be that the failure of CBS Cable does not mean that cultural programming has no future in the United States.

Whatever the future of cultural programming via cable, it cannot be denied that public television stations are in poor financial shape. In 1982 they successfully persuaded Congress not to authorize the cuts that the Reagan administration had proposed both for Media Projects and for the budget of the Corporation for Public Broadcasting, which funnels money to public television stations and to independent producers for operations and productions. But many officials of public television stations believe it is highly unlikely, at least for the next ten years, that federal funds for public television will increase, so they are looking for other ways of raising funds.

Putting a limited number of commercials on the air is one possibility. According to Fred Flaxman, assistant general manager for a public television station in Tucson, "A new system of financing public television that includes limited commercials could eliminate annoying 16-day on-air membership drives. . . . It would eliminate direct corporate influence of program choices, and would increase the funds available for high-quality program production. . . . It would do all this with reduced federal funding and without ever interrupting a program for ads."[51] Some public-television officials, including Lawrence K. Grossman, president of Public Broadcasting Service, are afraid that commercials would make public television into a different kind of system. "We're here to serve," Grossman has said, "not sell."[52] Michael Kinsley, the editor of *Harper's,* disagrees. While admitting that "a lot of public TV is very good,"

Kinsley argued in 1983 that "as cable and other technological developments make it easier to serve minority tastes at a profit, it's going to get harder to see why my particular minority taste [his interest in cultural programming] should be subsidized by the government." According to Kinsley, "Public broadcasting would be well advised to abandon the non-commercial pretext."[53]

The need for federal support is not easy to determine, yet the case for increased support for Media Projects should be based primarily on need, not on whether NEH has supported the production of valuable or well-received programs in the humanities in the past. What about past programming? Bennett has implied that NEH's record in Media Projects is poor, complaining that some projects lay outside the humanities, some were "ideological tirades passing as the humanities," and others were weak and undeserving of support.[54] A look at the various efforts supported by Media Projects, though, reveals few that appear to be "ideological tirades." On the contrary, NEH's emphasis on the collaboration of scholars and filmmakers has led to the production of programs tending toward the bland. In short, NEH's record in the area of the media is a satisfactory one. The agency has supported the production of many good programs—and a few truly outstanding ones.

MUSEUMS, HISTORICAL ORGANIZATIONS, AND LIBRARIES

The case to be made for cutting that portion of the NEH budget for support of museums is weaker than that for cutting back on Media Projects. For one thing, the commercial world has not entered the museum business to the extent that it has the field of cultural programming via the media. For another, museums and historical organizations (if not libraries), as many observers have pointed out, have been effective in the diffusion of humanistic knowledge—if effectiveness is defined as reaching a broad public. In 1980 Duffey reported to Congress that NEH-supported interpretive exhibits developed and presented by museums and historical organizations were reaching twenty-eight to thirty million people each year.[55] These statistics are more definitive than those for State Programs because they are based on actual counts of people entering museums.

The growing popularity of museum-going can be explained in part by recent transformations in many museums, especially those devoted to art. From repositories which in many ways were intimidating to all but art historians and connoisseurs, they become institutions intent on attracting large numbers of relatively affluent and well-educated college graduates who are interested in art and culture in general but are not particularly knowledgeable about art history. One observer has called this new museum constituency neither high-brow nor low-brow but "new-brow."[56] The museums catering to these people have shed their austere atmosphere; they are now more than likely to be lively and brash, often borrowing techniques successfully used by department stores for dramatic displays of the art and artifacts that are often part of highly publicized special exhibits, commonly called "blockbusters." In some ways a visit to a major exhibition at an art museum is like a visit to a large department store on one of its busiest days. Today's museums are often noisy and crowded, and art historians and connoisseurs are apt to find them vulgar and disagreeable. Perhaps they are, but at the same time they are much less forbidding to those who are not well versed in high culture. Many Americans now regard visiting a museum with the family (including small children) as an ordinary weekend event, akin to going on a picnic.

The growth in museum attendance, as well as the growing number of museums and historical organizations (more than 750 museums have been founded since 1969), would probably have occurred had NEH and NEA never existed, since the burgeoning ranks of "new-brows" are interested not only in art but also in history, especially American social history. Nevertheless, NEH support has contributed to this growth in several ways. Exhibitions such as "The Treasures of Tutankhamen," "The Splendor of Dresden," and "Pompeii: 79 A.D.," all of which were sponsored in part by NEH, have lured millions of people to museums, many of them, in all probability, for the first time. With the help of NEH's Challenge Grants Program, many museums have held fund-raising drives to pay for expanding their physical plants or improving their services. Finally, NEH has given small planning grants to a number of museums and historical organizations to help them evaluate their collections and plan exhibits.

Having abetted the dissemination of culture in general, especially art and history, NEH's support for museums and historical organizations would appear to be a success story. Yet some informed observers have questioned specific aspects of NEH policy, particularly the agency's insistence upon interpretative exhibits. For instance, according to Hilton Kramer, former chief art critic for the *New York Times*, an NEH-supported exhibit entitled "German Realism of the Twenties" was "afflicted with so many written explanations and catchpenny labels that what may have been intended as intellectual aids to the show end up as a wordy, obnoxious obstacle course distracting attention from the pictures on view."[57] And Serena Rattazi, an official at a New York State art museum, similarly complained in a recent article in the *New York Times* that interpretative materials intended to make art more accessible are a bad habit which "dangerously shifts the attention of the museum visitor away from the art work and on to the information *about* it."[58]

Has "the writing on the walls," as Mark Lilla put it, "clearly gotten out of hand in museums today?"[59] The *1980 Report* thinks not, for it recommends that museums "mount more exhibits informing visitors of the cultural, aesthetic, historical, and technical forces surrounding the creation of the objects displayed."[60] But Sherman Lee, the director of Cleveland's Museum of Art, believes otherwise. According to Lee, "Humanists don't understand that a work of art doesn't need words to accompany it. They tend to think that if you understand something through what you see rather than what you read, that it is witchcraft."[61]

But surely some exhibits, those that are primarily historical in nature, should include much "writing on the walls," whereas others, those that focus on works of art, should not. Because of its desire to distinguish itself from NEA, NEH has been inflexible about the question of interpretation, insisting that it will support only exhibits that rely heavily on interpretative materials. Some of the "writing on the walls" supported by NEH grants has been irritating, but as Marc Pachter, the historian of the National Portrait Gallery, has remarked, "We'll never solve completely to our satisfaction the problem of how much words, simply the presence of words, interfere with the perception of the object."[62]

NEH and other organizations that underwrite museum exhibitions have been criticized for yet another reason: their interest in "blockbuster" shows, which are sometimes more impressive for their showmanship than for their discrimination, taste, and understanding. According to Hilton Kramer, "The organizations that now sponsor museum shows, whether they are government agencies or corporate patrons, naturally prefer to lavish their money on the kind of block-buster event that will bring them a maximum 'return' on their investment—the return, in this case, being favorable and extensive publicity."[63] Other critics have complained that these shows stretch museum budgets and cause them to neglect permanent collections. These shows may also be "conditioning the public to expect lavish new shows on a regular basis."[64] John Walsh, Jr., the director of Boston's Museum of Fine Arts, does not share this disapproval of large-scale shows, believing that they enable museums to build up their attendance. According to Walsh, "Membership grows when popular exhibits are shown; once people have made that investment, you have a claim on them."[65] In any case, criticisms of "block-busters" apply more to corporate underwriters, for NEH has not favored large-scale grants, even though when it reports to Congress it dwells on the impact of the large-scale exhibits it has supported.

Some observers have been dismayed by the emphasis placed on numbers by both NEH and museums. "Increasing the number of people who come to museums is no measure of their success," Alan Shestack, the director of the Yale Art Gallery, points out.[66] True, but neither is it a measure of their failure. To take a negative view of the explosion in museum attendance, to argue that the transformation of museums has resulted not in the spreading of culture but in its trivialization, is to be excessively concerned about the obvious fact that some people who wander through a much-heralded exhibit get very little out of the experience. "Museum visiting," Neil Harris, a professor of American history at the University of Chicago, has said, "cannot be easily described by a generalization. Like books, exhibits are read at many levels and velocities."[67]

For all their lapses in taste, museums, whether of art, history, or science, are our most successful vehicle for the dissemination of cultural concerns because they represent the least condescending way of encouraging the lay public to become more knowledgeable about art, history, or—broadly speaking—high culture. Those who seek to learn something from what museums offer can do so at their ease and at their own pace. They are not lectured to in ways that make them feel anxious about their intelligence or lack of knowledge. In any case, as Mark Lilla has noted, "for some people of truly refined tastes, the writing on the museum wall . . . may be distracting and annoying, but the connoisseurs are free to do what they have always done."[68] They are free, that is, to ignore the paraphernalia that have caused the contemporary museum to resemble a department store.

Museums and historical organizations deserve some support from NEH, yet it is not altogether clear how much support they should be given. The agency's budget for this category has followed the same pattern as that for media projects. Begun in 1972 with less than $500,000, funding for museums and historical groups rose to more than $9.4 million in 1981, then was cut back to $6.9 million in 1982. The proposed budget for 1983 was only $3.6 million. Contemplating these deep cuts, Mamie Phipps Clark, president of Museums Collaborative, warned that "the Government would do well to avoid precipitous action if it values the preservation of our cultural heritage."[69]

It is highly unlikely, though, that the proposed cuts in NEH's support would seriously damage either museums in particular or our cultural heritage in general. The cuts would, of course, make it more difficult for NEH to underwrite large-scale exhibits, but such efforts are in any case likely to win corporate support: the spring 1983 exhibition at the Metropolitan Museum of Art in New York of art from the Vatican, for example, was supported mainly by the Philip Morris Corporation and received no support from either NEA or NEH. And some of the grants NEH has awarded in the past should probably have been made by state humanities committees or state tourist agencies instead. It is hard to envision, for example, why NEH should have awarded $102,000 to the North Carolina Department of Cultural Resources for the final editing, layout, and printing of 5,000 "Sourcebooks of Historical Places in North Carolina." It is equally hard to justify NEH's expenditures of $61,000 on production of a thirty-minute orientation film on the city of Cape May, New Jersey. Finally, some of NEH's grants to museums can be easily characterized as extravagant. The list of recent awards suggests areas in which the agency may have been too generous: $250,000 to the Puppeteers of America for an exhibit on the art of puppetry; $136,000 to the Cincinnati Fire Museum for the support of a permanent exhibit on the role of fire-fighting in the growth of Cincinnati; an impressive $430,000 to the Yakima Indian Nation to develop a National Museum of the Yakimas. It may be unfair to single out these grants as examples, but the generous funding given these projects implies that cuts in NEH's support for museums and historical organizations do not necessarily signify that the agency has lost interest in cultural dissemination. Such cuts could also mean NEH has decided that the private sector and museums themselves, by means of corporate grants and higher museum entrance fees, should absorb a greater share of the cost of cultural dissemination.

NEH support for museums and historical organizations touches indirectly on another question: How many museums do we need? The question is impossible to answer fairly, but those who object to cutbacks in NEH's support for museums, or to cutbacks in federal involvement in this area in general, imply that the more museums and historical organizations we have, the better. Mamie Phipps Clark has observed, with some justification, that "museums are responsible for transferring to succeeding generations a material record of human culture and the natural world. It is this collective cultural memory that assists living audiences to understand and measure change."[70] But it may be that the rapid growth of museums in the 1970s was excessive and that we are in danger of wallowing in the past, of getting lost in nostalgia, which Robert Nisbet has called the "rust of history."[71] If, owing to reduction in federal support, some museums were forced to close their doors, it would not necessarily mean we would be in danger of losing our cultural heritage.

Museums and historical organizations have proven themselves effective vehicles for cultural diffusion, but what about public libraries? In 1978 NEH began a program entitled "Humanities Projects in Libraries," which was intended to benefit libraries serving the adult public. The program began with a budget of $1.8 million, which had risen to $3.4 million by 1981. But the proposed budget for 1983 was only $500,000, and it is likely that the program will soon be discontinued as a separate effort.

It is undeniable that, in the words of the *1980 Report*, "the public library is the single most important cultural institution in most communities, and preserving its vitality is unequivocally in the national interest."[72] But NEH's library program has not appeared to do much to preserve the "vitality" of libraries, since it is specifically intended to stimulate the use of libraries by means of "thematic programs, exhibits, media, publications, and other library activities."[73] It had been NEH's hope that such events would lure into libraries people who were not normally accustomed to frequenting them, with the result that these newcomers would eventually become devoted library patrons. (Apparently only 30 percent of this country's adult population takes advantage of public libraries to a significant extent, and a quarter of that group accounts for three-quarters of adult use.) Yet given the nature and facilities of most libraries, it is doubtful that they will ever become popular places for exhibits or discussion groups. NEH's program is well-meaning, but it encourages libraries to become involved in activities—such as the creation of materials for exhibits and the staging of exhibits—that are extraneous to their main purpose and of only limited help in alleviating their financial woes.

OTHER PUBLIC PROGRAMS

In its sixteen-year history NEH has awarded a number of grants to organizations not primarily in the business of cultural dissemination. Most of these grants have been made by the Division of Special Programs. Within a category of support called Program Development Grants, Special Programs has supported projects that sought to bring the humanities to "new groups in the population, such as labor unions, ethnic groups, and national adult membership organizations."[74]

Many of the grants made within this category have been subject to criticism. For example, the Heritage Foundation, a public policy research institute based in Washington and with ties to the Reagan administration, declared in 1981 that "it is in this area that most of the politically motivated funding originates,"[75] implying that under Duffey NEH had deliberately sought to reward traditional Democratic constituencies—in short, that Duffey politicized the agency. Most of the complaints focused on grants made to several labor unions, including the Amalgamated Clothing and Textile Workers Union (ACTWU), District 1199 of the National Union of Hospital and Health Care Employees, and the National Association of Office Workers, but there was also sharp criticism of a grant to the Foreign Policy Association (FPA) for the support of discussion groups on contemporary foreign policy issues.

Much of this criticism was misguided or simply uninformed. The Foreign Policy Association, to take but one instance, received several grants from NEH under both the Berman and Duffey chairmanships, and the fact that the FPA chose to discuss SALT II when President Carter was seeking this treaty's ratification was in no way a result of pressure on the part of NEH to do so. NEH has never had a hand in determining the FPA's agenda. In retrospect, it was probably a poor idea for NEH to award grants to an organization engaged in clarifying current issues of foreign policy simply because no fostering of the humanities was involved. But it is a mistake to imply that NEH, at the behest of the Carter administration, awarded the grant to the Foreign Policy Association in order to drum up public support for the SALT II treaty.

It is equally unfair to accuse Duffey of political partisanship simply because NEH awarded several grants to labor unions under his chairmanship. Many of the preliminary staff meetings that eventually led to NEH grants to unions were held during Berman's chairmanship. The agency deliberately sought out unions and other national organizations in order to convince Congress, and particularly Senator Pell, that it was doing its utmost to abet the dissemination of culture as well as to loosen its ties with academe. These grants may have been political in the sense that NEH hoped by making them to win friends in Congress, but they were by no means the product of partisan political calculation. Many members of the NEH staff wholeheartedly believed that awarding funds to unions and other national organizations would be an effective way of gaining new audiences for the humanities.

The disputed grants have had their champions as well as their critics. According to Jack Golodner, executive director of the AFL-CIO's Department for Professional Employees, they have helped union members, especially younger ones, familiarize themselves with American history: "We now recognize that a whole generation has grown up without understanding its roots. That doesn't bode well for the labor movement, or for the society."[76] Duffey, echoing Golodner's remarks, claimed, "These programs don't just serve the union, they serve the whole society. When people behave without a sense of history, it's a threat to the entire country."[77]

Precisely what "sense of history" are those who attend such programs likely to obtain? Most of the programs developed by unions with NEH support seem designed either to instill in workers pride in the past achievements of their unions or to foster appreciation of the extent to which unions help their members cope with contemporary problems. In short, the programs are designed to bolster support for unions among the rank and file, especially among younger workers. As Joyce D. Miller, vice-president and director of social services for the ACTWU, remarked about her union's grant: "It's brought members closer to the union. . . . The programs seem to have awakened their interest in [it]."[78] It is perfectly understandable why unions choose to reflect with pride on their accomplishments, but is it wise for NEH to support programs that are only peripherally related to the humanities?

To question the wisdom of awarding grants to labor unions is not of course to suggest that NEH should ignore the role of unions in American history. But it is unlikely that labor history will be well served by grants to unions. It is doubtful, for example, that the National Association of Office Workers, which was awarded a grant of $200,000 to set up a curriculum on the history of office workers, will produce exemplary humanistic materials. Duffey himself, in remarks made at the announcement of this grant, implied that the cultural concern of the National Association of Office Workers was not so much humanistic inquiry as consciousness-raising. He spoke of the grant as if it were a contribution to a worthwhile cause—raising the status of office workers, many of whom are stuck in "low paying, low status jobs."[79] The curriculum produced by such an organization is likely to be tendentious and self-serving, which would also be the case if the grantee were a business organization such as the National Association of Oil Producers.

Even if the materials resulting from this grant were exemplary, the fact that they were produced by a union (or a business organization) would probably deprive them of a wide audience. Duffey has argued that "the story of the working lives of Americans is a part of our history that hasn't been fleshed out by historians,"[80] and it has been largely overlooked by the general public as well. Precisely because his point is valid (although it is important to note that in recent years historians have begun to work in the field of labor history), NEH should fund labor history programs mainly at established cultural institutions. Such programs would presumably attract broader audiences for labor history than unions ever could. While the agency should stop short of ruling out grants to unions or other national membership organizations, it should refrain from encouraging applications from them or, for that matter, from organizations representing ethnic groups. Such organizations are likely to produce materials that are long on celebration and short on critical inquiry.

The several grants NEH has made to urban consortia to develop a variety of programs examining the multifaceted histories of particular cities are quite another matter. These projects, which have taken place in Houston, Hartford, Baltimore, Birmingham, Philadelphia, San Antonio, and elsewhere, are celebratory in the best sense: they instill in city residents a sense of civic pride in the distinctive histories of their cities.[81] Moreover, these projects, which usually combine the arts and the humanities in ways that make them both informative and entertaining, raise citizens' awareness of the cultural complexity, resulting from the presence of diverse ethnic strains, which characterizes most cities. Yet it is not altogether obvious why such projects should require substantial support from NEH, since ideally they should be able to raise funds from local foundations and corporations as well as from the cities themselves. If NEH does support such projects, it should be through state humanities committees or by means of the challenge grant mechanism.

NEH has also ventured, in a modest way, into the field of continuing education. Its two main efforts in this area have been grants to the State University of New York at Albany to develop the Capital District Humanities Program and to the National Council on the Aging to establish its Senior Center Humanities Program. Both projects, which offer courses and discussion groups that meet in libraries, community centers, apartment complexes, and nursing homes, appear firmly grounded in the humanities, and thus can serve as model projects to test whether or not there is a strong general interest in adult education in the humanities. If these projects are successful in recruiting students, then other universities and organizations, following suit, will no doubt begin to offer courses in the humanities, for, as one observer has put it, "colleges and other institutions are waging a pitched marketing battle for the part-time tuition dollar."[82] Perhaps the most sensible thing for NEH to do in this area is to continue to sponsor, as it has in the past, regional workshops to explore ways in which humanities courses can be designed to be of interest to adults with no particular background in the humanities.

In trying to market humanities courses for adults, educational institutions may be tempted, as the *1980 Report* warned, to cheapen and vulgarize the discipline.[83] But there is an even greater danger—condescension, the assumption that adults are primarily interested only in questions that directly affect their lives. Such an assumption leads adult-education planners to assign books on old age to old people or books about labor history to workers. The *1980 Report* argues that "if continuing education in the humanities is to thrive, educational institutions must continually identify the interests of adult learners."[84] But such an objective calls for educational institutions to design courses that will enable people to develop new interests, courses that will, in effect, take people out of themselves, which is, after all, what education is supposed to do. Educational institutions should not assume that adults cannot read "difficult" books, such as the masterpieces of Western civilization, and those who design courses for adults should not patronize the poorly educated by allowing humanities courses to become mere discussion groups in which the elderly reminisce about the past or discuss how their values differ from their neighbors' or their grandchildren's. Adult-education courses cannot be as rigorous as high-level graduate courses, but they should not be so watered-down that they fail to challenge those taking them.

NEH's Fellowships and Seminars for the Professions was one program for adults that successfully avoided condescension. Overseen by the Fellowships Division, the program offered intensive four-week summer seminars for businessmen, journalists, labor leaders, lawyers, doctors, and educational administrators. In addition, the program offered nine-month fellowships for journalists at either Stanford or the University of Michigan. Unlike the division's seminars, these fellowships were relatively unstructured, with fellows designing their own courses of study (mainly but not exclusively in the humanities) and required only to attend weekly seminars on the humanities. Begun in 1972, the program was repeatedly attacked as a boondoggle by Senator William Proxmire of Wisconsin, Washington's self-appointed fiscal watchdog, and as a result was abolished in 1982, except for seminars for journalists.

In many ways this program was especially vulnerable. In 1978 Senator Proxmire accused NEH of spending $2 million in the previous year for grants to "well-heeled doctors, lawyers, and school administrators to attend tuition-free, vacationlike, month-long humanistic bull sessions at some of the choicest vacation spots in the country."[85] It may be difficult to justify the nine-month fellowship for journalists, which offered, as the director of the Stanford Program put it, "an opportunity for fresh air, new ideas, different perspectives." If journalists need nine months off in order to acquire "different perspectives,"[86] why not such a program for police officers, military officers, politicians? The four-week seminars, however, seem to have been more carefully thought out and more rigorous. Taught by leading scholars in the humanities, they required participants to do a significant amount of serious reading to help them clarify some of the difficult questions facing them in daily professional practice. In 1983 NEH said that it would not finance the program for journalists after 1983-84, but the program at Stanford will continue, having received a $4 million grant from the Knight Foundation. Since the four-week seminars were highly regarded by those who attended them, NEH should consider reinstituting them, with at least half the cost for the seminars to be met either by those attending them or by other sponsoring organizations.

Finally, NEH has sponsored several programs that are difficult to categorize, including Youth Programs and Courses by Newspaper. The former is intended "to stimulate the active participation of young people in humanities projects,"[87] and most of its awards go to individuals between the ages of sixteen and twenty-four for a wide variety of projects in the humanities. The assumption behind the program is that, if young people are given the chance to oversee projects of their own design, many will go on to professional scholarly work. It may be, however, that people in this age group would be better served by learning more about the humanities than by "doing" the humanities, so to speak.

The Courses by Newspaper project, which was run by the University Extension of the University of California at San Diego, consisted of adult education college-credit courses that required enrollees to read a series of column-length articles appearing in newspapers throughout the nation. "Energy and the Way We Live," for example, appeared in 512 newspapers and was offered as a credit course at 355 community colleges. According to George A. Colburn, director of the program, Courses by Newspaper was designed less as an innovative experiment in adult education than as an attempt to persuade newspapers to offer "exciting news features on significant and timely subjects"[88] written by qualified academic scholars. Since the project failed to stimulate a groundswell of interest on the part of newspapers in hiring scholars as regular columnists, NEH declined to supply Courses by Newspaper with additional funding after its first eight years. In any case, the articles bore a close resemblance to similar articles appearing regularly on Op-Ed pages or in weekly and monthly journals of opinion.

To complete this survey of NEH's efforts in the public's behalf, we must mention the support that the agency, in conjunction with the Ford Foundation, has given for the creation of the Library of America, a not-for-profit corporation devoted to the publication of moderately priced editions of major American works of literature and history. Modeled on the French *Editions de la Pléiade* (published by Gallimard), each book is handsomely printed on acid-free paper. The Library of America, which plans to publish more than a hundred volumes, has been praised for making available to the general public works that either have been out of print or have been published in poor-quality paperback editions. Yet Hugh Kenner has questioned the choices of writers for inclusion in the series, singling out a volume devoted to three novels by Harriet Beecher Stowe. Moreover, he doubts that the volumes will be as widely used as their French counterparts, since they are heavier and less portable than the *Pléiade* editions.[89] Furthermore, because of copyright problems, the Library of America will rarely be able to publish major works by twentieth-century American writers.

The audience for most Library of America books will probably be small because of the high prices charged. It is unlikely, for instance, that many Americans will pay $25 (or $19.95 by subscription) for a volume of Washington Irving's writings. Yet some volumes may do well—for example, the one containing Henry James's complete criticism, which has never before been available in a single volume. Whatever its eventual level of sales, the project is noteworthy because it focuses on books that will last a lifetime. By contrast, most other materials produced by NEH-supported projects attempting to diffuse the humanities—oral history tapes, slide shows, pamphlets, photos, brochures—have been of little lasting value.

The Library of America was, of course, a no-risk venture for NEH; it came blessed with the approval of leading American scholars in the humanities. There was little danger that the project would turn out badly. In its attempts to diffuse the humanities NEH has occasionally taken chances on more daring projects, some of which have been poorly received, but perhaps it has not stuck its neck out often enough or far enough. The agency has not, for the most part, encouraged projects that challenge the adult public to grapple with the major works of civilization. Quoting Samuel Johnson, Paul Fussell, a participant in many public programs, has said that "a desire for knowledge is the natural feeling of mankind; and every human being whose mind is not debauched will be willing to give all that he has to get knowledge."[90] It is difficult to generalize about the wide variety of public programs that NEH has supported, but it seems as if many of them presume their audiences to be limited, if only in the sense that they are interested solely in their own experiences, in what they already know. As Robert Hollander has said, "the working supposition of too many people, in Washington and at the state level, is that the 'real humanities' are beyond the ken of the great unwashed public. This is simply not true. The audience is there if we but seek to find it."[91] Instead of trying to cater to the present interests of the adult public, NEH should try to enable adults to move beyond the horizons of their own inevitably limited experiences.

9

Conclusions
and Recommendations

IN 1965 Frederick Burkhardt, president of the American Council of Learned Societies, was fully confident of the "tremendous impact [a humanities foundation] would have on the intellectual and artistic life of our country. In a few years this . . . foundation would invigorate the humanities . . . at every level of our education system and in our society generally."[1] Eighteen years and more than a billion dollars later, the National Endowment for the Humanities has had no such impact. It would be easy to leap to the conclusion that the agency has been less than a great success.

Certainly "the humanities" has not become a household term, and there is little prospect that it ever will. Indeed, the general public is (in the words of Gordon Ray, president of the Guggenheim Foundation) "largely indifferent" to the humanities.[2] But the failure of humanistic studies to gain currency with the public is less significant than the state of the humanities within the nation's educational system. In the early 1980s most observers believed the humanities to be in a bad way in the nation's schools, colleges, and universities. Research in this area was suffering, they claimed, owing to a dearth of teaching jobs at the college level that led many would-be scholars to choose other professions. And many were concerned about the physical deterioration of books and other materials in the nation's major research libraries, as well as about the financial plight of these libraries. In short, most knowledgeable observers would agree with the *1980 Report,* which expressed "a profound disquiet about the state of the humanities in our culture."[3]

Is NEH, then, an out-and-out failure? Judged by the inflated claims of those who lobbied for the creation of a national humanities foundation in the 1960s, it might indeed deserve this description. In retrospect, though, it was unrealistic to expect that an agency with a relatively small budget could ever have a strong and lasting impact on American culture. The budgets of NEH and the National Endowment for the Arts together constitute less than 10 percent of the amount spent annually for the support of the humanities and the arts by both private and public sources in this country.[4] In any case, "the fate of the humanities in America is somewhat different than the immediate fate of . . . NEH,"[5] an obvious but nevertheless important point made by Joseph Duffey in 1981.

If the humanities are in trouble in the United States, the fault lies not so much with NEH as with what Flaubert called "the atmosphere." "Have you ever remarked," Flaubert wrote to Louise Colet in the mid-nineteenth century, "how all authority is stupid concerning Art? Our wonderful governments (kings or republics) imagine that they have only to order work to be done, and it will be forthcoming. They set up prizes, encouragements, academies, and they forget only one thing, one little thing without which nothing can live: *the atmosphere*."[6] In the case of NEH the word connotes not only the sorry financial circumstances of humanistic institutions and the career crisis that set in during the 1970s, but also the attitudes of scholars, educators, and even the general public. This atmosphere in America in the past two decades has worked against NEH's mission, making its venture seem at times almost quixotic. Those decades could be described as a period in which educators were preoccupied with innovation and scholars were bent on cultivating their own gardens, both neglecting to fight for a rigorous curriculum. And the general public, or at least that part of the public taking an interest in educational policy, seemed more concerned about equity than about excellence. As Gordon Ray has observed, "Government support or the lack of it is not at the heart of the problem of the humanities. Their welfare depends primarily on reading, on teaching, on the preservation of liberal education."[7]

While NEH cannot be held responsible for the atmosphere surrounding the humanities, those who lobbied for its founding may have made it more difficult for the agency to change the attitudes and opinions of Americans. They did not, after all, make the case for a national humanities foundation that they originally wanted to make: that such a foundation should be structured on the model of the National Science Foundation. Assuming that Congress would not vote to establish an agency dedicated mainly to institutionalized scholarship in the humanities, these early supporters obviously believed they had chosen the only possible strategy, since it is not easy to make a strong case for federal support of humanistic research. Robert Lumiansky has remarked, "Sometimes I think we ought to have the American Council of Learned Societies sponsor a contest every three months for the best statement explaining and justifying the humanities to the public."[8] Nevertheless, if those who originally lobbied for the establishment of NEH, as well as those who have since taken a strong interest in its work, had defended its existence on the Madisonian grounds that "Learned Institutions ought to be favorite objects with every free people,"[9] they might have had less trouble with Congress in the long run. Certainly there would have been less need to belabor, as Ronald Berman thought he had to do for the benefit of Senator Pell, the obvious point that "it is very difficult to avoid funding academic enterprises."[10] And the constant need to reiterate the caveat that NEH should not be compared with NEA might have been avoided as well.

There is some danger, however, in making too much of the rhetoric that led to the establishment of NEH as well as the overheated defenses of the humanities found in the *1964 Report* and, to a lesser degree, in the *1980 Report*. This point was well illustrated recently by Suzanne Garment, a columnist for the *Wall Street Journal,* who, after criticizing most general defenses of NEH and the humanities as smacking of "vulgarity, mediocrity, and plain political partisanship," acknowledged "the good that specific Endowment grants had done for specific libraries and pieces of research."[11] Clearly the work NEH has supported speaks more highly for the continuing existence of the agency than the arguments that NEH itself and other spokesmen for the humanities have made in its defense. In order to evaluate this work, we must ignore the rhetoric in which the agency has swaddled itself and assess the relative worth of the various programs it administers.

But by what criteria can we fairly assess the worth of a given program, especially if that program has for the most part supported a series of discrete projects? In 1979 NEH established an Office of Evaluation and Assessment Studies to support "studies which document and assess present and projected needs and conditions in the humanities" as well as those "which evaluate how effectively or efficiently current programs are meeting those needs."[12] Yet, as we have seen, needs are far from easy to assess, and as the 1970 minority report of the House subcommittee responsible for NEH's authorization acknowledged, "there can never be enough federal aid, realistically speaking, to satisfy all the claimed needs of the many different segments of the arts and the humanities."[13] As difficult as it is to assess needs, it is even more difficult to translate them into dollar amounts and assign them an order of importance. NEH has from time to time provided support for studies attempting to evaluate the needs of the humanities—the report, for example, entitled *Scholarly Communication*—but invariably these studies come to the same conclusion: more federal money, not less, is needed. Spokesmen for the humanities would be well served by reminders, like that of an observer in the *New Republic,* that "what's missing [in their claims] is any trace of humble acknowledgment that they are also necessarily competing for federal money with others far needier than they."[14]

This is not to say that we should dismiss the notion of needs altogether, for some needs in the world of the humanities are relatively evident, and it is in the public interest for NEH to meet them. There is an obvious need, for example, for more funding for graduate fellowships in both the humanities and the sciences, since "a decline in the quality of graduate teaching and research may be the most serious long-term threat to the nation's internal and external strength."[15] NEH should offer a substantial number of annual fellowships for outstanding students who wish to pursue doctorates in their chosen fields. Unlike NSF, NEH has never offered graduate fellowships, mainly because Senator Pell has been adamantly opposed to them, but it makes no sense to support scholarship in the humanities without ensuring that the continuity of scholarship is maintained.

There is also an evident need for aid to the nation's major research libraries, especially the independent research libraries, to help them meet mounting operating costs as well as to prevent their collections from deteriorating. There is a pressing need as well for funds to support the editing and publication, and hence the preservation, of the writings of American statesmen, especially the Founding Fathers.

Although NEH's main concern should be strengthening America's "learned institutions" in the broadest sense, it should not be afraid to take risks in support of maverick scholars or unusual projects. According to Richard Sennett, the director of the New York Institute for the Humanities, the humanities are in trouble because they have become "too academic."[16] Sennett underestimates the problem; the humanities are in trouble for many reasons. But it would be unfortunate if NEH were to regard the humanities as the exclusive preserve of academe, and it would be equally unfortunate if the agency were to refrain from funding unusual projects—for example, in prisons—for fear of arousing controversy.

Education, as well as research and preservation, is an area of manifest need. NEH should support beleaguered high school teachers by expanding its summer institutes program, and should give aid to colleges with weak humanities programs. At the same time, the agency should bear in mind that a direct grant is not necessarily the best way to help the humanistically needy. It may be, for example, that a model project developed by a major university will do more to help a small liberal-arts college in need of bolstering its curriculum in the humanities than would a direct grant to that small college.

NEH should also undertake a reappraisal of the humanities curriculum. E.D. Hirsch, Jr., a professor of English at the University of Virginia, spoke recently of the need for a "pluralist curriculum" in literature: "If we want a pluralist curriculum in the United States, the way to get one is to appoint a pluralistic national body and ask them to hammer out curricular compromises, and give us curricular guides that actually name authors and works."[17] Some observers may object that, if NEH were to support the production of such guides, it would loom too large on the landscape of the humanities. But guides offered by scholarly bodies convened by NEH would not in any sense be official. Rather, they would serve as concrete starting points for discussing the question of what high school and college students should study.

Three other areas of the curriculum need to be explored: history, science for the nonscientist, and civics. Bernard Bailyn has said that "the great proliferation of historical writing has served not to illuminate the central themes of western history but to obscure them."[18] NEH might profitably ask historians to wrestle with the difficult question of what should go into the history curriculum for all students, not only those majoring in history. And Michael Sovern, president of Columbia University, has pointed out that we consider it a national scandal that young people cannot write a clear sentence, yet we tolerate "with remarkable equanimity a similar inability to know what it means to think scientifically."[19] NEH should look carefully at the important question of what nonscientists ought to learn about science. Finally, according to a recent report of the Carnegie Foundation, schools and colleges need to update and restore "the tired old academic workhorse 'civics' . . . to an honored place" in the curriculum, since "we are becoming civically illiterate. Unless we find better ways to educate ourselves *as citizens,* we run the risk of drifting unwittingly into a new kind of Dark Age—a time when small cadres of specialists will control knowledge and thus control the decision-making process."[20]

Whatever the level of NEH's appropriations, the issue of whether or not the agency's budget is sufficient to meet the needs of the humanities will always be a matter of controversy. Debate about the relative needs of different program areas will also continue. But despite NEH's claim that it always seeks to address needs, this criterion does not seem to have been a major factor in many of NEH's policy decisions. What specific need was met, for example, when NEH created the program area entitled State, Local and Regional Studies? Why do teachers need funds to plan new courses? Is it appropriate to invoke the criterion of need when considering public programs that were created in response to congressional prescription, not to public demand? In this last case, it was largely Senator Pell's conviction that the public needed humanities programs to improve the quality of life in the United States that prompted NEH's response in the area of public programs. Perhaps Pell was justified in arguing that the general public needed the humanities, but the need he invoked seems far less compelling than that of, for example, the New York Public Library for funds to meet its operating expenses.

The question of need is complicated by the potential role of the private sector in meeting the humanities' needs, either by itself or in conjunction with NEH through the agency's challenge grants. The issue of private support for the humanities came into full view in 1981, when the Reagan administration argued that reduced federal support for both the arts and the humanities would undoubtedly be compensated for by the private sector. In making its argument the administration alleged that growth in federal support tends to dry up private support, a claim that was less than convincing, since private support had grown right along with federal. In 1967, for instance, business contributed $22 million to the arts, whereas in 1980 the figure was $436 million.[21] Most observers agreed with Representative Paul Simon of Illinois, who decried the Reagan administration's cuts, claiming that "far from supplanting private and corporate dollars, this federal money spurs private and corporate support that otherwise would not exist."[22] The controversy was difficult to resolve because reliable data on private support for the humanities and the arts—particularly the humanities—did not exist. As was noted in *Humanities Report,* "There was no good method to substantiate or deny the administration's contention that individuals, foundations, and corporations would provide additional support when public funding was reduced."[23]

Estimating private support for the humanities is complicated because different schemes of classification are used by organizations that compile data on philanthropic giving. Most such schemes lump the arts and the humanities together, although some support for the humanities is subsumed under the category of support for education. The American Association of Fund-Raising Council recently reported that, in 1981, $3.3 million out of a total of $53.6 billion for philanthropy in the United States went to the arts and the humanities,[24] but most observers believe that the lion's share of this money has gone to the arts. (Corporations, which in 1979, for the first time in the nation's history, exceeded foundations in philanthropic giving, appear to give less to the humanities than foundations do.) In the early 1980s NEH began systematically to organize existing information about foundation support for the humanities in order to evaluate, as an NEH official put it, whether "we are going against the grain of the private sector or complementing it by funding regions that don't get much funding."[25] The task is a difficult one, since the agendas of foundations change, sometimes suddenly, and levels of corporate support are affected by the state of the economy and current tax laws.

There remains individual giving (also, of course, affected by the economy and by tax laws), a resource that has remained largely unexploited by humanistic institutions, although colleges, universities, and museums have relied heavily on individual donors for general support. In recent years some research institutions, notably the New York Public Library and the Folger Shakespeare Library in Washington, D.C., have mounted campaigns to raise funds from individual donors. Individual giving, as Gordon Ray has suggested, "may yet play a significant role."[26] Corporations likewise "have a much larger capacity to increase their contributions than do foundations."[27] Ray's point, presumably, is that under the new tax law, enacted in 1981, the amount of net corporate income that can be deducted for charitable donations increased from 5 to 10 percent. But it is unlikely that support from corporations, foundations, or individuals will increase dramatically in the near future.

NEH has never ignored the private sector. Its matching-grants formula was devised to gain private support for individual projects, and its challenge grants, which began in 1977, were implemented to "foster the development of continuing non-federal support for the nation's humanities institutions." By 1983, according to NEH, 586 nonprofit institutions had been awarded challenge grants. These institutions have gained more than $560 million in gift and matching funds, $125 million of which came from NEH.[28] The program has won wide approval. James M. Morris of the Mellon Foundation has said, "I would like to think that the challenge grants would be the last program that the administration would want to cut."[29]

Officers of corporations and foundations have often admitted that they depend upon NEH's peer review process to guide them in choosing which proposals to fund among the many they receive. This means that if NEH has previously approved a particular institution's request for a challenge grant, then that institution is apt to be viewed as more worthy of private support than another that has neither gained, nor perhaps even sought, NEH approval. But some corporate and foundation officials dislike this arrangement; they feel that they are being put on the spot by prospective grantees who come to them with NEH's seal of approval. It would obviously be disturbing if a significant amount of private support for humanistic institutions were validated by NEH, with corporations, foundations, or even individual donors relying upon NEH to tell them which humanistic institutions are most worthy of support.

Although NEH has always stressed its efforts to meet the needs of the humanities, in recent years it has dwelled more heavily on its own impact. In 1980 an NEH report argued that "notwithstanding its limited resources, the Endowment has over time enabled significant numbers of Americans to participate in humanistic activities."[30] Yet what do the figures displayed in this report mean? We learn, for example, that "the Education Division programs have reached an estimated 7,000 humanities teachers and 250,000 of their students annually," and that "the number of students whose humanities educations have been substantially improved due to Endowment grants has climbed into the millions."[31] Surely these claims should be treated skeptically, since we cannot generalize about the quality of NEH's grants to improve the teaching of the humanities. The agency has, of course, no choice but to toss numbers around when it tries to persuade Congress that it is doing a commendable job. But the resort to numbers is a kind of whistling in the dark, a way of maintaining that NEH's efforts have had a positive effect despite the "profound disquiet" about the state of the humanities in American culture expressed by so many observers.

Time and again we have encountered key words that have played a central part in the ongoing debate about NEH: needs, imbalance, visibility, impact, and, in the late 1970s, representation. Unfortunately, there has not been enough talk about excellence. How many excellent things—books, movies, exhibits, courses, whatever—have come into existence as a result of NEH support? Why is the word "excellent" often regarded with suspicion as a conservative rallying cry? There is nothing necessarily elitist about the pursuit of excellence. The Founding Fathers assumed that, because Americans were opposed to a society based on privilege, they would honor excellence regardless of rank and seek out men and women capable of excellence from all walks of life. If NEH has not dwelled sufficiently on excellence, the fault lies not only with the agency but also with the temper of the times. In the 1970s many people placed excellence in opposition to equity, as if a society that sought out and honored excellence was somehow unjust. NEH could help to reaffirm its commitment to excellence by offering not one but at least ten awards annually to outstanding individuals in the humanities. The awards should go not only to scholars but also to teachers and librarians.

Yet if excellence has not been sufficiently championed by NEH, neither should it be made the sole criterion for awarding grants. Need, no matter how difficult it is to define, must also be taken into account. NEH should concentrate its attention on the humanistically needy, so to speak—or to put it another way, should try to aid those who, whether as scholars, as teachers, or as both, are hampered in their pursuit of excellence.

NEH might be better able to clarify and address the basic needs of the humanities if it made several basic structural and institutional changes. The agency should reorganize its Divisions of Research Programs and Fellowships Programs to emphasize the distinction between research and preservation. There should be a Division of Research that would support the production of scholarship, and a Division of Scholarly Resources that would support work currently done within the Research Materials and the Research Resources programs. Within the newly organized Division of Research, there should be two categories of support: Fellowships for Senior Humanists (over thirty-five or forty) and Fellowships for Younger Humanists. The two-track category is necessary because it is difficult for younger scholars, who have perhaps published only a couple of articles or one book, to compete with senior scholars, who have often published a great deal. Fellowships for younger humanists should be awarded by means of blind reviewing, in order to prevent reviewers from discriminating in favor of those who teach at major universities. This kind of review, however, would not be appropriate for the selection of senior fellowship recipients, since reviewers should know whether senior applicants have good track records as productive scholars.

Other changes, relatively simple to execute, may also be useful. NEH should consider, for example, instituting advisory committees similar to those employed by NSF. These committees would evaluate all categories of support every three years, especially categories of support for research. And the agency could eliminate a good deal of unnecessary staff work by having the National Council review proposals only over a certain amount—say, $250,000.

NEH should also consider making more substantial changes. First, the agency should no longer administer the state humanities committees. Although William Bennett has tried to tighten NEH's grip on these committees, it is unlikely that the agency will ever be able to win effective control over them. NEH's attempt to keep close watch on the doings of the state committees is bound to fail, since NEH simply does not have enough staff to do so. As things now stand, the state committees are justified in grumbling, as some have, that NEH's supervision of their programs is often arbitrary and high-handed, since it is based on a poor knowledge of the programs.

Second, the agency, through the mechanism of the National Council, should look into the question of how the chairman is selected. Surely there is a better way to do this. While the agency should not be insulated from the political process, a cloud of suspicion now hangs over the chairmanship: the suspicion that, because he is chosen by the president, the NEH chairman will make grants for partisan reasons. By contrast, the head of the British academy, elected annually by the fellows of the academy, is both insulated from the political process and unlikely to feel constrained to pay homage to the policies of any party. The day-to-day work of the academy is the responsibility of an individual whom this institution calls its secretary. Since this means that the head of the academy is not expected to give up his research while in office (he is elected annually), the academy generally chooses a scholar of high distinction—Sir Isaiah Berlin, for example, was president for several years— to fill this office. NEH might use the British system as a helpful model on which to base recommendations for changes in its present chairman selection procedures.

The final—and most radical—recommendation to emerge from this analysis of federal support for the humanities and NEH is that Congress should consider a major reorganization of federal agencies so that most federal support for cultural dissemination is housed in one agency. The new agency would embrace the work of NEH's General Programs (with the exception of Humanities Projects in Media, which should probably be folded into the Corporation for Public Broadcasting), NEA, the Institute of Museum Services, and perhaps certain programs of the Smithsonian Institution. Such a reorganization would enable NEH to rid itself of a difficulty that has plagued it from the outset: trying to support teaching and scholarship as well as to make an impact on the general public.

This reorganization would make the pattern of federal support for the humanities more closely resemble the French and British models. Briefly, cultural dissemination in France is mainly the responsibility of the Ministry of Culture and Communication, whereas support for research, not only in the humanities but also in the sciences, falls primarily under the aegis of the Centre National de la Recherche Scientifique. (In France the operative terms are not the sciences and the humanities but *les sciences exactes* and *les sciences humaines*.) In Britain, cultural dissemination comes within the purview of the British Arts Council; research in the humanities is primarily the responsibility of the British Academy, an independent organization constituted by royal charter in 1902, which receives most but not all of its funds from the government (in 1977-78 approximately 15 percent of the income of the academy was from private sources).

The point of reorganization would not, of course, be simply to imitate the French or British patterns but to find the most effective way to foster humanistic scholarship, effective teaching, and diffusion of the humanities. The current arrangement has made it all too easy for congressmen and independent observers alike to introduce criteria, such as impact, distribution, and representation, that hamper NEH's efforts to support research and improve teaching. Moreover, this arrangement has led NEH to exaggerate the distinction between public programs in the humanities and those in the arts. If cultural dissemination were the responsibility of a Department of Cultural Affairs, a more coherent, efficient, and successful policy of support for museums and historical societies might be fashioned. It is not simply that NEH, as now constituted, tries to do too much, as that its different mandates tend to work at cross purposes to one another, so that the agency is pulled in two directions, that of NEA and that of NSF. In my view the latter direction is the appropriate one.

Finally, NEH should not be afraid of becoming more forceful in attempting to shape the humanities, or at least in trying to draw attention to particular problems that beset them. One of the fears raised by those opposed to the founding of the agency has not been borne out: it has not become a ministry of culture. And the structure of the Endowment as well as its relatively small budget make it unlikely that it will ever loom ominously large in the world of the humanities.

NOTES

Introduction

1. "Thoughts on Humanistic Scholarship and Teaching in the 1980's and 1990's," *ACLS Newsletter* 33 (Winter–Spring 1982): 7.

2. *Washington Post*, Mar. 11, 1980, p. D1.

3. Ibid., Oct. 8, 1979, p. C8.

4. *Fat City: How Washington Wastes Your Taxes* (South Bend, Ind.: Regnery/Gateway, 1980), p. 136.

5. "Welfare Arts," *Public Interest* 53 (Fall 1978): 136.

6. "Should the Government Subsidize the Arts?" *Policy Review* 10 (Fall 1979): 67.

7. *New York Times*, Nov. 26, 1980, p. C1.

8. *The Humanities in American Life* (Berkeley: Univ. of California Press, 1980), p. 163. (Hereafter cited as *1980 Report*.)

9. *Newsweek*, Mar. 16, 1981, p. 31.

10. Joseph Conrad, *Nostromo* (New York: Modern Library, 1951), p. 582.

Chapter 1

1. U.S., Congress, Senate Committee on Labor and Public Welfare, House Committee on Education and Labor, Joint Hearings, *Bills to Establish National Foundations on the Arts and Humanities*, 89th Cong., 1st sess. (Feb. 23 and Mar. 3, 1965), p. 627. (Hereafter cited as Joint Hearings, *Arts and Humanities Bills*.)

2. Editorial, *Science*, July 31, 1964, p. 449.

3. D.S. Greenberg, "Humanities: Proposals to Set Up a National Foundation Are Gathering Support in the House and Senate," *Science*, Jan. 15, 1965, pp. 273–74.

4. "Foundation on the Arts and Humanities," *Congressional Quarterly Almanac* (1965), p. 624.

5. *Congressional Record*, 89th Cong., 1st sess. (Mar. 10, 1965), p. 4594.

6. John Higham, "The Schism in American Scholarship," *Writing American History: Essays on Modern Scholarship* (Bloomington: Indiana Univ. Press, 1970), p. 4.

7. *Congressional Record*, 89th Cong., 1st sess. (June 10, 1965), p. 13107.

8. *Report of the Commission on the Humanities* (New York: American Council of Learned Societies, 1964), p. 6. (Hereafter cited as *1964 Report.*)

9. *Congressional Quarterly Almanac* (1965), p. 625.

10. *New York Times*, June 28, 1964, sec. 4, p. 7.

11. David Boroff, "A Plea to Save the Liberal Arts," *New York Times Magazine*, May 10, 1964, p. 18.

12. Submitted for the record in Joint Hearings, *Arts and Humanities Bills*, p. 217.

13. Trilling cited in Ann Hulbert, "The Humanities Hustle," *New Republic*, Dec. 6, 1980, p. 38; Frye cited in Laurence Veysey, "The Humanities in American Universities since the 1930's: The Decline of Grandiosity" (paper delivered to the Society for Humanities, Cornell Univ., Ithaca, N.Y., Nov. 29, 1979), p. 28.

14. Cited in Daniel J. Kevles, *The Physicists: The History of a Scientific Community in America* (New York: Knopf, 1978), p. 385.

15. Cited in ibid.

16. Ibid., p. 410.

17. Ibid., p. 395.

18. Cited in ibid., p. 393.

19. Lionel Trilling, "The Leavis-Snow Controversy," in *Beyond Culture* (New York: Viking Press, 1968), p. 163.

20. Norman Podhoretz, *Breaking Ranks: A Political Memoir* (New York: Harper and Row, 1979), p. 117.

21. *1964 Report*, p. 111.

22. *New York Times*, Mar. 11, 1965.

23. *Ibid.*, Aug. 16, 1964, sec. 4, p. 7.

24. *1964 Report*, p. 4.

25. Ibid., p. 119.

26. Charles Blitzer, "The Plight of the Humanities in Hard Times," in *Government and the Humanities: Toward a National Cultural Policy*, ed. Kenneth W. Tolo (Austin, Texas: Lyndon B. Johnson School of Public Affairs, 1979), p. 107.

27. *1964 Report*, pp. v–vi.

28. Joint Hearings, *Arts and Humanities Bills*, p. 215.

29. Veysey, "Humanities in American Universities," p. 3.

30. *1964 Report*, p. 3.

31. Greenberg, "Humanities," p. 274.
32. Joint Hearings, *Arts and Humanities Bills*, p. 105.
33. *1964 Report*, p. 10; Joint Hearings, *Arts and Humanities Bills*, pp. 104, 228.
34. *Congressional Quarterly Almanac* (1965), p. 623.
35. Ibid. (1964), p. 428.
36. Ibid. (1965), p. 624; *New York Times*, Jan. 7, 1965, p. 27.
37. *Congressional Quarterly Almanac* (1965), p. 624.
38. Blitzer, "Plight of the Humanities," p. 107.
39. *1964 Report*, p. 10.
40. Joint Hearings, *Arts and Humanities Bills*, p. 107.
41. Ibid., p. 372.
42. Mary Lynn Kotz, "John Brademas: The Unquestioned Leader, the Energizer, the Touchstone of the Arts," *Art News*, Sept. 1980, pp. 90-96.
43. Blitzer, "Plight of the Humanities," p. 107.
44. Charles Blitzer, "Remarks Prepared for a Meeting of the Presidential Task Force," *ACLS Newsletter*, Summer–Fall 1981, p. 5.
45. Higham, "Schism in American Scholarship," p. 21; Strayer cited in Howard Mumford Jones, *American Humanism* (New York: Harper and Row, 1957), p. 81.
46. Higham, "Schism in American Scholarship," pp. 24, 7.
47. U.S., Congress, House, Hearings before the House Committee on Education and Labor, *Bills to Establish National Foundations on the Arts and Humanities*, 89th Cong., 1st sess. (Feb. 24 and Mar. 22-24, 1965), p. 387.
48. Joint Hearings, *Arts and Humanities Bills*, p. 108.
49. *Congressional Record*, 89th Cong., 1st sess. (June 10, 1965), p. 13111.
50. Ibid., Sept. 15, 1965, p. 23957.
51. Ibid., p. 23973.
52. Ibid., p. 23946; *Congressional Quarterly Almanac* (1965), p. 626.
53. *Congressional Record*, Sept. 15, 1965, p. 23942.
54. *Congressional Quarterly Almanac* (1965), p. 626.
55. *Congressional Record*, Sept. 15, 1965, p. 23941.
56. Ibid., p. 23945.
57. Joint Hearings, *Arts and Humanities Bills*, p. 109; *Congressional Record*, Sept. 15, 1965, p. 23944.
58. *1964 Report*, pp. 6, 12; Greenberg, "Humanities," p. 274.
59. Joint Hearings, *Arts and Humanities Bills*, p. 109; *Wall Street Journal*, article cited by Representative Paul Findley in *Congressional Record*, Sept. 15, 1965, p. 23949.
60. "The Ph.D. Meat Market," *Newsweek*, Feb. 4, 1980, p. 74.
61. Cited in Chester E. Finn, Jr., *Scholars, Dollars and Bureaucrats* (Washington, D.C.: Brookings Institution, 1978), p. 23.
62. See NEH, *Second Annual Report*, p. 18.
63. *Congressional Record*, Sept. 15, 1965, p. 23951.

64. Joint Hearings, *Arts and Humanities Bills*, p. 371.

65. Marvin Meyers, ed., *The Mind of the Founder* (Indianapolis, Ind.: Bobbs-Merrill, 1973), p. 440.

CHAPTER 2

1. NEH, *Second Annual Report*, p. 9.
2. NEH, *First Annual Report*, p. 2.
3. NEH, *Fourth Annual Report*, p. 6.
4. NEH, *Third Annual Report*, p. 37.
5. NEH, *Sixth Annual Report*, p. 43.
6. NEH, *Fifth Annual Report*, p. 31.
7. NEH, *Fourth Annual Report*, p. 4.
8. Ibid., p. 12.
9. NEH, *Seventh Annual Report*, p. 7.
10. *NEH Program Announcement, 1981-82*, p. 28.
11. NEH, *Eighth Annual Report*, p. 62.
12. Ibid.
13. *NEH Program Announcement, 1981-82*, p. 28.
14. Ibid., p. 29.
15. U.S., Congress, House, Committee on Education and Labor, *Hearings for the Reauthorization of the National Foundation for the Arts and the Humanities*, 96th Cong., 2d sess. (Feb. 6, 1980), p. 133. (Hereafter cited as *1980 House Reauthorization Hearings*.)
16. *New York Times*, May 31, 1982, p. C9.
17. *Humanities Report*, May 1982, p. 14.
18. *New York Times*, May 31, 1982, p. C8.
19. *Wilson Library Bulletin*, Sept. 1982, p. 23; *Washington Post*, Nov. 18, 1982, p. E9.
20. *Wilson Library Bulletin*, Sept. 1982, p. 23.
21. *Washington Post*, June 9, 1983, p. C1.

CHAPTER 3

1. *New York Times*, Oct. 16, 1977, sec. 2, pp. 1-2.
2. Ibid.
3. Ibid.
4. Ibid.
5. Ibid., Nov. 13, 1977, sec. 2, p. 5.
6. *Chronicle of Higher Education*, Jan. 17, 1977, p. 5.
7. U.S., Congress, Senate Committee on Labor and Public Welfare, House Committee on Education and Labor, Joint Hearings, *U.S. Humanities and Cultural Affairs Act of 1975*, 94th Cong., 1st sess. (Nov. 12, 1975), p. 205.
8. *Congressional Record*, Senate, 93d Cong., 1st sess. (May 1, 1973), p. 8078.
9. U.S., Congress, Senate Committee on Labor and Public Welfare,

House Committee on Education and Labor, Joint Hearings, *Amendments to the National Foundation on the Arts and Humanities Act,* 91st Cong., 2d sess. (Jan. 20, 1970), p. 79. (Hereafter cited as *1970 Joint Reauthorization Hearings.*)

10. *Chronicle of Higher Education,* Jan. 12, 1976, p. 10; Oct. 1, 1976, p. 4.

11. *Congressional Record,* Senate, 95th Cong., 1st sess. (Sept. 12, 1977), p. S14709.

12. *New York Times,* Aug. 22, 1977, p. 22.

13. *Chronicle of Higher Education,* Jan. 12, 1976, p. 10.

14. U.S., Congress, House, Committee on Appropriations, *Hearings on Appropriations for Department of Interior and Related Agencies for 1980,* 96th Cong., 1st sess. (May 8, 1979), p. 829. (Hereafter cited as *1980 Appropriations Hearings.*)

15. *New York Times,* June 28, 1977, p. 1.

16. *Chronicle of Higher Education,* May 14, 1979, p. 1.

17. U.S., Congress, House, *House Appropriations Hearings for 1981,* 96th Cong., 2d sess. (Apr. 10, 1980), p. 216. (Hereafter cited as *1981 Appropriations Hearings.*)

18. Ibid., p. 225.

19. Unpublished report of the House Appropriations Committee, Subcommittee on the Department of Interior and Related Agencies (Mar. 23, 1979), p. 12.

20. *1981 Appropriations Hearings,* p. 269.

21. Ibid., p. 218.

22. Ibid., p. 224.

23. Ibid., p. 268.

24. Ibid., p. 270.

25. Cited in Kevles, *The Physicists,* p. 404.

26. *1981 Appropriations Hearings,* p. 217.

27. *Chronicle of Higher Education,* Sept. 19, 1977, p. 3.

28. Robert Coles, "The Humanities and Human Dignity," *Change* 10 (Feb. 1978): 9, 63.

29. Joseph Duffey, "The Social Meaning of the Humanities," *Change* 12 (Feb./Mar. 1980): 40.

30. "NEH after 15 Years," *ACLS Newsletter* 31 (Spring 1980): 3.

31. *New York Times,* Oct. 16, 1977, sec. 2, p. 2.

32. *1980 House Reauthorization Hearings,* p. 209.

33. NEH, *Thirteenth Annual Report,* p. 6.

34. "Open Letter to Michael Joyce," Dec. 1, 1980 (distributed to members of NEH's National Council and to NEH staff), p. 6. Joyce wrote the Heritage Foundation's 1980 report on the NEH.

35. NEH, *NEH and Hispanics* (1979).

36. *1980 House Reauthorization Hearings,* p. 144.

37. *Congressional Record,* House, 96th Cong., 2d sess. (Nov. 17, 1980), p. H10899.

38. NEH, *Thirteenth Annual Report,* p. 5.

39. *New York Times,* June 28, 1977, p. 1.
40. *Congressional Record,* House, 94th Cong., 2d sess. (Jan. 4, 1978), p. E7256.
41. "Moving the Humanities into the Penthouse," in Tolo, *Government and the Humanities,* p. 8.
42. *1980 Appropriations Hearings,* p. 124.
43. U.S., Congress, Senate, Committee on Labor and Public Welfare, *Nomination of Ronald S. Berman to Be Chairman of the National Endowment for the Humanities,* 94th Cong., 2d sess. (Sept. 15, 1976), p. 582. (Hereafter cited as *1976 Senate Nomination Hearings.*)
44. *New York Times,* June 28, 1977, p. 1.
45. Garment cited in C. Richard Swaim, "The National Endowment for the Arts: 1965-1980," in *Public Policy and the Arts,* ed. Kevin V. Mulcahy and C. Richard Swaim (Boulder, Colo.: Westview Press, 1982), p. 185.
46. *New York Times,* Jan. 18, 1974, p. 24.
47. Inserted by Senator Charles Percy in *Congressional Record,* 95th Cong., 1st sess. (Apr. 5, 1977), p. S5593.
48. *New York Times Magazine,* Apr. 28, 1974, p. 94.
49. Robert Brustein, "Trashing the Endowments," *New Republic,* Nov. 22, 1980, p. 26.
50. *Humanities Report* 1 (May 1979): 13-14.
51. Cited in William Brennan, "Second Thoughts about First Principles: The Federal Humanities Program" (paper distributed by the Federation of Public Programs in the Humanities, 1980), p. 7.
52. *Humanities Report* 2 (Oct. 1980): 4.
53. *Time,* May 10, 1982, p. 102.
54. Cited by Jonathan Yardley, "Back to the Humanities," *Washington Post,* May 17, 1972, p. C1.

CHAPTER 4

1. NEH, *Sixteenth Annual Report,* p. 5.
2. Ibid., p. 6.
3. National Science Foundation, *Grants for Scientific and Engineering Research* (NSF 81-79), p. 8.
4. National Science Foundation, *Peer Review and Guidelines for the Selection of Projects,* Circular No. 132, p. 1.
5. National Endowment for the Arts, *Annual Report,* 1981, p. 5.
6. *1976 Senate Nomination Hearings,* p. 42.
7. *1980 Appropriations Hearings,* p. 1036.
8. Statistics taken from *Digest of Educational Statistics, 1980* (Washington, D.C.: National Center for Educational Statistics); from *Summary Reports of Doctorate Recipients from United States Universities for the Years 1972 to 1979* (Washington, D.C.: National Research Council of the National Academy of Sciences); and from *1980 Fact Book for Academic Administration* (Washington, D.C.: American Council on Education).

9. *1980 House Reauthorization Hearings,* p. 78.
10. Ibid.
11. Hook's letter is dated Jan. 28, 1981; Duffey's letter, Feb. 12, 1981. Copies made available by NEH.
12. See Deborah Shapley, "Peer Review: Under Attack and Changing," *Humanities Report* 1 (Jan. 1979): 10.
13. Unpublished response to 1979 House Appropriations Committee Report, March 1979, p. 20. (Distributed by NEH to the House Committee.)
14. See *Chronicle of Higher Education,* Jan. 12, 1981, p. 3; *New York Times,* Jan. 6, 1981, p. C1.
15. J. Brian Hyland and C.R. Anderson, "House Appropriations Committee Report: Vol. II, NEH" (Washington, D.C., Mar. 23, 1979, unpublished), pp. 13-15.
16. *1980 Appropriations Hearings,* p. 704.
17. U.S. Congress, Senate, *Arts, Humanities and Museum Services Act of 1979,* 96th Cong., 1st sess. (June 27, 1979), p. 704. (Hereafter cited as *1979 Senate Reauthorization Hearings.*)
18. Ibid., p. 225.
19. Wray Herbert, "Blind Refereeing," *Humanities Report* 2 (Apr. 1980): 6.
20. *1976 Senate Nomination Hearings,* p. 48.
21. NEH, *Sixteenth Annual Report,* p. 6.
22. Cited in Joseph A. Harriss, "While You're Up, Get Me a Grant," *Reader's Digest,* June 1981, p. 171.
23. *Review Processes: Assessing the Quality of Research Proposals* (Washington, D.C.: National Commission on Research, 1980), p. 8.
24. *Chronicle of Higher Education,* Apr. 23, 1980, p. 8.
25. Ibid., Nov. 18, 1981, p. 23.
26. *1980 House Reauthorization Hearings,* p. 151.
27. Stephen Cole, Leonard Rubin, and Jonathan R. Cole, "Peer Review and the Support of Science," *Scientific American* 237 (Oct. 1977): 34.

CHAPTER 5

1. *Humanities Report* 2 (Jan. 1980): 14.
2. *The Basic Writings of George Washington,* ed. Saxe Commins (New York: Random House, 1948), pp. 569, 649.
3. Cited in Russell Blaine Nye, *The Cultural Life of the New Nation, 1776-1830* (New York: Harper and Row, 1960), p. 72.
4. *Senate Nomination Hearings 1976,* p. 23.
5. *1980 House Reauthorization Hearings,* p. 66.
6. *Review Processes: Assessing the Quality of Research Proposals* (Washington, D.C.: National Commission on Research, 1980), p. 1.
7. *1970 Joint Reauthorization Hearings,* p. 7.
8. NEH, *Third Annual Report,* p. 43.

9. Ibid.

10. *1980 Appropriations Hearings,* p. 806.

11. NEH, *Eighth Annual Report,* p. 62.

12. Ibid.

13. NEH, *Fifth Annual Report,* p. 62.

14. NEH, *Sixth Annual Report,* p. 43.

15. NEH, *Seventh Annual Report,* p. 7.

16. Ibid., p. 33.

17. *Review Processes,* p. 9.

18. Joseph Duffey, "The Climate for Research" (speech given at Western Michigan Univ., Oct. 1, 1979), p. 3.

19. William May, *The Humanities and the Civic Self* (Bloomington: Poynter Center of Indiana Univ., 1979), p. 14.

20. U.S., Congress, Senate Committee on Labor and Public Welfare, House Committee on Education and Labor, Joint Hearings, *Arts and Humanities Amendments of 1967,* 90th Cong., 1st sess. (July 12, 1967), p. 29.

21. *Washington Star,* Apr. 22, 1981, p. A18.

22. *Chronicle of Higher Education,* July 13, 1981, p. 48.

23. Ibid., Nov. 24, 1982, p. 9.

24. Ibid.

25. *1970 Joint Reauthorization Hearings,* p. 78.

26. *1980 Report,* p. 103.

27. *1980 House Reauthorization Hearings,* p. 66.

28. *The Politics of Aristotle,* ed. and trans. Ernest Barker (London: Oxford Univ. Press, 1978), p. 57.

29. *Wall Street Journal,* Jan. 10, 1980, p. 22.

30. "NEH: After 15 Years," *ACLS Newsletter* 31 (Spring 1980): 9.

31. *Review Processes,* p. ix.

CHAPTER 6

1. NEH, *Second Annual Report,* p. 23.

2. *1964 Report,* pp. 33, 41-42.

3. *1980 Report,* p. 98.

4. Ibid., p. 93.

5. National Enquiry into Scholarly Communication, *Scholarly Communication* (Baltimore: Johns Hopkins Univ. Press, 1979), pp. 1, 20.

6. Elliott J. Echelman, "Research Libraries Face a Technology-Oriented Future," *Humanities Report* 3 (Dec. 1981): 4.

7. Warren J. Haas, "Research Libraries and the Dynamics of Change," *Scholarly Publishing* 11 (Apr. 1980): 195.

8. Daniel Boorstin, "Welcoming Remarks," *A National Preservation Program: Proceedings of the Planning Conference* (Washington, D.C.: Library of Congress, 1980), p. 12.

9. *Washington Post,* Mar. 25, 1981, p. B3.

10. *1980 Report,* p. 112.

11. *1980 Reauthorization Hearings,* p. 72.

12. NEH, *Seventh Annual Report,* p. 41.

13. NEH, *Overview of Endowment Programs for 1983-84,* p. 13.

14. U.S., Congress, Senate Committee on Labor and Public Welfare, House Committee on Education and Labor, Joint Hearings, *National Foundation on the Arts and Humanities Amendments of 1973,* 93rd Cong., 1st sess. (March 6, 1973), p. 738. (Hereafter cited as *1973 Joint Reauthorization Hearings.*)

15. Ibid., p. 797.

16. *1980 Reauthorization Hearings,* p. 73.

17. Ibid.

18. *1973 Joint Reauthorization Hearings,* pp. 797-98.

19. *1979 Senate Reauthorization Hearings,* p. 248.

20. Joseph Duffey, "Scholarship and Society: A Case for the Public Interest," *ACLS Newsletter* 29 (Spring 1978): 11.

21. See Imre T. Jarmy, "Editor's Notes," *National Preservation Report* 1 (Apr. 1979): 3-7.

22. *Wall Street Journal,* Oct. 26, 1982, p. 56.

23. Richard Severo, "Acid Devours Books," *New York Times,* Dec. 1, 1981, pp. C1, C4.

24. Boorstin, "Welcoming Remarks," p. 11.

25. *Proceedings of the Conference on the Research, Use and Disposition of Senators' Papers* (Washington, D.C.: U.S. Senate, 1978), p. 38.

26. Ibid., p. 57.

27. Michael Kammen, "The Historian's Vocation and the State of the Discipline in the United States," in *The Past Before Us: Contemporary Historical Writing in the United States,* ed. Kammen (Ithaca, N.Y.: Cornell Univ. Press, 1980), p. 34.

28. J.H. Hexter, "History and the Social Sciences," *Doing History* (Bloomington: Indiana Univ. Press, 1971), p. 109.

29. *Use and Disposition of Senators' Papers,* pp. 39-40.

30. Cited in Herbert T. Hoover, "Oral History in the United States," in Kammen, *Past Before Us,* p. 400.

31. *Use and Disposition of Senators' Papers,* pp. 75-76.

32. "Research Libraries and the Humanities," *Minutes of the Ninety-Fifth Meeting of the Association of Research Libraries* (Washington, D.C.: Association of Research Libraries, 1980), pp. 30, 32.

33. David S. Landes and Charles Tilly, eds., *History as Social Science: History Panel of the Behavioral and Social Sciences Survey of the National Academy of Sciences and the Social Science Research Council* (Englewood Cliffs, N.J.: Prentice-Hall, 1971), pp. 138-39.

34. "Libraries Need Advice of Scholars," *Humanities Report* 2 (Mar. 1980), 3.

35. "Foreword" to Kammen, *Past Before Us,* p. 13.

36. Haas, "Research Libraries and the Dynamics of Change," pp. 201-02.

37. Landes and Tilly, *History as Social Science*, p. 139.
38. *Chronicle of Higher Education*, Mar. 7, 1982, p. 11.
39. "The Role of Independent Research Libraries in American Society," *ACLS Newsletter* 31 (Summer–Fall 1980): 9.
40. *Scholarly Communication*, p. 50.
41. Jonathan Walters, "National Archives in Peril," *Humanities Report* 4 (Mar. 1982): 4.
42. See *Washington Post*, Jan. 22, 1982, p. A13.
43. Richard De Gennaro, "Research Libraries Enter the Information Age," *Library Journal*, Nov. 15, 1979, pp. 2407, 2410.
44. Cited in Echelman, "Research Libraries," p. 5.
45. *New York Times*, Mar. 14, 1982, sec. 1, p. 64.

CHAPTER 7

1. *1964 Report*, p. 6.
2. Ibid., p. 12.
3. Ibid., p. 20.
4. Ibid., p. 29.
5. *1970 Joint Reauthorization Hearings*, p. 95.
6. *Washington Post*, Oct. 14, 1981, p. A25.
7. *1980 Report*, p. 25.
8. *1980 House Reauthorization Hearings*, p. 60; *Humanities* 2 (Feb. 1981): 11.
9. *New York Times*, May 16, 1982, p. E8.
10. "American Education Revives," *Wall Street Journal*, July 7, 1982, p. 27.
11. Carnegie Council on Policy Studies in Higher Education, *Three Thousand Futures: The New Twenty Years for Higher Education* (San Francisco: Jossey-Bass, 1980), p. 130; idem, *Missions of the Curriculum: A Contemporary Review with Suggestions* (San Francisco: Jossey-Bass, 1977), p. 15.
12. *Fifth Report of the National Council on Educational Research* (Washington, D.C.: National Institute of Education, 1980), p. iii.
13. Fund for the Improvement of Post-Secondary Education, *The Comprehensive Program: Information and Application Procedures, 1981*, pp. 2-3, 6.
14. Finn, "American Education Revives."
15. J. Myron Atkin, "The Government in the Classroom," *Daedalus* 109 (Summer 1980): 97.
16. David G. Savage, "The Federal Schoolhouse," *New Republic*, Apr. 18, 1981, p. 23.
17. Daniel L. Duke, *The Impact of Trying to Make an Impact, or the Negative Side of Noble Ambitions*, Occasional Paper no. 7 (Stanford: Stanford Center for Research and Development in Teaching, 1980), p. 7.
18. Savage, "Federal Schoolhouse," p. 22.

19. *1980 Report*, p. 43.

20. NEH *Eighth Annual Report*, p. 40; Geoffrey Marshall, "Humanities Education in the 80s," *Humanities* 1 (Sept./Oct. 1980): 16.

21. *New York Times*, July 13, 1982, p. C1.

22. Lumiansky cited in George W. Bonham, "The Discomfited Humanities," *Change*, Mar. 1978, pp. 10-11.

23. *1964 Report*, p. 136.

24. *1980 Report*, p. 45.

25. Christina M. Kraus, "President's Panel Bewails Nation's Foreign Language Disability," *Humanities Report* 2 (Jan. 1980): 4.

26. Review of Paul Simon's *The Tongue-Tied American*, in *Washington Post Book World*, Nov. 16, 1980, p. 9.

27. *Washington Post*, July 16, 1981, p. 5.

28. *Research Universities and the National Interest: A Report from Fifteen University Presidents* (New York: Ford Foundation, 1981), p. 118.

29. National Council on Foreign Language and International Studies (New York, 1980), unpaginated.

30. See *Humanities* 1 (Sept./Oct. 1980): 16.

31. *Chronicle of Higher Education*, Sept. 22, 1980, p. 9.

32. Evaluator's report obtained from NEH (Grant No. ES-37120-77-344, Jan. 15, 1980).

33. See *New York Times*, Aug. 4, 1981, p. C3.

34. Cited in Kraus, "President's Panel," p. 5.

35. *Chronicle of Higher Education*, Jan. 12, 1981, p. 14.

36. *New York Times*, Aug. 4, 1981, p. C3.

37. *Chronicle of Higher Education*, Jan. 12, 1981, p. 1.

38. *Newsweek*, Nov. 15, 1982, p. 99C.

39. *1964 Report*, pp. 138-39.

40. Clifton Fadiman and James Howard, *Empty Pages: A Search for Writing Competence in School and Society* (Belmont, Cal.: Fearon Pitman, 1979), pp. 9-10.

41. John Brereton, "Learning from the Writing Crisis," *Teachers College Record* 80 (Dec. 1978): 358.

42. NEH, *Eleventh Annual Report*, p. 33.

43. *1980 House Reauthorization Hearings*, p. 61.

44. Fadiman and Howard, *Empty Pages*, p. 132.

45. Cited in ibid., p. 18.

46. Council for Basic Education, "Comments on the Third National Writing Assessment," News Release (Washington, D.C., Jan. 16, 1981).

47. *Time*, May 19, 1980, p. 88.

48. *1964 Report*, p. 25.

49. Ibid., p. 117.

50. Ibid., p. 114.

51. *1980 Report*, pp. 44-45.

52. Cindy Ris, "Why Johnny Doesn't Know His History," *Wall Street Journal*, Oct. 29, 1980, p. 23.

53. Cited in ibid.

54. Cited in ibid.

55. *1980 Report*, p. 45.

56. Descriptions of projects obtained from NEH.

57. *Humanities* 1 (Sept./Oct. 1980), p. 18.

58. Robert Darnton, "Intellectual and Cultural History," in Kammen, *Past Before Us*, p. 333.

59. Kammen, "Historian's Vocation," p. 43.

60. Cited in Hazel Whitman Hertzberg, "The Teaching of History," in Kammen, *Past Before Us*, p. 500.

61. *1980 Report*, p. 165.

62. Savage, "Federal Schoolhouse," p. 22.

63. Dorothy Wickenden, "How Schools Succeed," *New Republic*, Apr. 18, 1981, p. 14.

64. *Chronicle of Higher Education*, Dec. 1, 1982, p. 1.

65. Ibid., p. 12.

66. Diane Ravitch, "American Education: Has the Pendulum Swung Once Too Often?" *Humanities* 3 (Nov. 1982): 1.

67. *Chronicle of Higher Education*, Dec. 1, 1982, p. 1.

68. A. Bartlett Giamatti, "The American Teacher," *Harper's*, July 1980, p. 28.

69. *1980 Report*, p. 50.

70. *Washington Post*, Oct. 4, 1979, p. A24.

71. *1980 Report*, p. 52.

72. *New York Times*, July 20, 1982, p. C4.

73. Ibid.

74. *1980 Report*, p. 48.

75. Boyer cited in Albert Shanker, "Morale Low, 'Best Are Bailing Out'" (advertisement), *New York Times*, Feb. 21, 1982, p. E9.

76. *Washington Post*, Sept. 30, 1982, p. A3.

77. Diane Ravitch, "Colleges: Where Are Their Standards?" *Washington Post*, July 18, 1981, p. 18.

78. Tyler cited in Finn, "American Education Revives."

79. *Washington Post*, Mar. 2, 1981, p. B1.

80. Ibid., p. B4.

81. *Wall Street Journal*, Jan. 22, 1981, p. 1.

82. Ibid., p. 22. See also Denis Doyle and Marsha Levine, "Private Meets Public: An Examination of Contemporary Education," *Meeting Human Needs: Toward a New Public Philosophy* (Washington, D.C.: American Enterprise Institute, 1982), pp. 272-329.

83. *New York Times*, Dec. 28, 1982, p. C1.

84. *Newsweek*, Oct. 25, 1982, p. 129.

85. *New York Times*, May 8, 1983, p. E18.

86. *Washington Post*, June 6, 1983, p. A2.

87. Victor Fuchs, "Educational Reform Begins at Home," *Wall Street Journal*, June 17, 1983, p. 26.

88. Ibid.

CHAPTER 8

1. See *Washington Post,* Dec. 9, 1982, p. 8; *New York Times,* Dec. 9, 1982, p. 1.

2. *Washington Post,* Dec. 9, 1982, p. 8.

3. *New York Times,* Mar. 11, 1981, sec. 3, p. 25.

4. Moira Egan, "The NEH Budget Request: A Mixed Blessing," *Humanities Report* 4 (Mar. 1982): 18.

5. *Congressional Record,* Senate, 96th Cong., 2d sess. (June 21, 1979), p. S8253.

6. "A Brief History of the State Humanities Programs," in *Citizens, Scholars and the Humanities: An Introduction to State Humanities Programs* (Minneapolis: Federation of Public Programs in the Humanities, 1980), p. 34.

7. Cited in Charles Trueheart, "State Humanities Committees," *Humanities Report* 1 (Mar. 1979): 11.

8. *Congressional Record,* Senate, 96th Cong., 2d sess. (June 21, 1979), p. S8253.

9. Ibid.

10. "A Brief History," p. 32.

11. *Washington Star,* June 28, 1979, p. B1.

12. See Trueheart, "State Humanities Committees," p. 12.

13. *1980 Report,* p. 173.

14. "A Brief History," pp. 34-35.

15. John Barcroft, "The Three Threats to State Programs," in *Citizens, Scholars and the Humanities,* p. 114.

16. Charles Frankel, "Why the Humanities," in Tolo, *Government and the Humanities,* p. 23.

17. Cited in Trueheart, "State Humanities Committees," p. 13.

18. Robert Hollander, "State Committees Should Emphasize 'Real Humanities,'" *Humanities Report* 4 (Feb. 1983): 2-3.

19. See James Smith and Rudi Anders, "1976 and After: 'New Directions' for State Programs," in *Citizens, Scholars and the Humanities,* pp. 37-46.

20. Richard Wasserstrom, "'Justification' and State Humanities Programs," in *The Views from Montaigne's Tower: Essays on the Public Uses of the Humanities,* ed. Michael Sherman (Minneapolis: Federation of Public Programs in the Humanities, 1980), p. 17.

21. *1980 Report,* p. 110.

22. Charles Frankel, "The Philosopher," *Proceedings of the National Meeting of State-Based Committees* (1973), p. 50.

23. Barcroft, "Three Threats to State Programs," p. 113.

24. *1980 House Reauthorization Hearings,* p. 50.

25. Donna Shoemaker, "State Committees in Maine and Oklahoma Enter a Second Decade," *Humanities Report* 3 (Mar. 1981): 11.

26. Cited in Trueheart, "State Humanities Committees," p. 13.

27. Charles S. Cole, Jr., *Effective Learning: A Study of Innovative Pub-*

lic Humanities Programs (Minneapolis: Federation of Public Programs in the Humanities, 1980), p. i.

28. Ibid., p. 1.

29. Trueheart, "State Humanities Committees," p. 13.

30. William C. Havard, "Scholarly Standards and Public Humanities Programs" (paper distributed by the Federation of Public Programs in the Humanities, 1982), pp. 15-16.

31. Barbara Delman Wolfson, "State of the State," *Humanities* 3 (Dec. 1982): 14.

32. Cited in Fraser Barron's newsletter, *Government and the Arts* (Sept. 1982), p. 7.

33. Ibid., Nov. 1982, p. 9.

34. William Brennan, "Second Thoughts about First Principles," p. 57.

35. Ibid., pp. 57-58.

36. NEH, *Second Annual Report*, p. 14.

37. Brooke Gladstone, "Endowment Media Fund Loses $3M," *Current*, Sept. 30, 1982, p. 1.

38. *New York Times*, Mar. 11, 1981, sec. 3, p. 25.

39. Ibid., Sept. 30, 1979, sec. 2, p. 1.

40. *1980 Report*, p. 144.

41. Jay Ruby, "Scholars and Filmmakers," *Humanities* 1 (Mar./Apr. 1980): 14.

42. *Humanities Projects in Media* (NEH brochure, 1981), p. 5.

43. Cited in Gladstone, "Endowment Media Fund Loses $3M."

44. Ibid.

45. John J. O'Connor, "What Lies Ahead for Cultural Programming?" *New York Times*, Dec. 12, 1982, p. H33.

46. *Washington Post*, Sept. 16, 1982, p. C1.

47. O'Connor, "What Lies Ahead?"

48. *Washington Post*, Sept. 16, 1982, p. C1.

49. Ibid., p. C14.

50. *Newsweek*, Sept. 27, 1982, p. 66.

51. *Wall Street Journal*, May 15, 1981, p. 23.

52. Ibid., Mar. 10, 1982, p. 24.

53. Michael Kinsley, "None Dare Call It Commercial," *Harper's*, Mar. 1983, p. 13.

54. Gladstone, "Endowment Media Fund Loses $3M."

55. *1980 House Reauthorization Hearings*, p. 54.

56. Mark Lilla, "Art and Anxiety: The Writing on the Museum Wall," *Public Interest* 66 (Winter 1982): 40.

57. Hilton Kramer, "Revelations of the Weimar Era," *New York Times*, Oct. 5, 1980, p. D32.

58. Rattazzi cited in Lilla, "Art and Anxiety," p. 50.

59. Ibid., p. 49.

60. *1980 Report*, p. 128.

61. Cited in Jonathan Walters, "Art Exhibits and Design," *Humanities Report* 3 (Oct. 1981): 6.

62. Cited in ibid.

63. Hilton Kramer, "When the Size of the Show Determines the Content," *New York Times,* Dec. 7, 1980, p. D3.

64. Walters, "Art Exhibits and Design," p. 5.

65. Cited in ibid.

66. *Newsweek,* Oct. 15, 1979, p. 129C.

67. Neil Harris, "The Exhibition as Text," *Humanities* 3 (Apr. 1982): 8.

68. Lilla, "Art and Anxiety," p. 52.

69. Mamie Phipps Clark, "Museums' Options," *New York Times,* July 21, 1981, p. 15.

70. Ibid.

71. *Sociology as an Art Form* (New York: Oxford Univ. Press, 1978), p. 83.

72. *1980 Report,* p. 133.

73. *NEH Program Announcement, 1981-82,* p. 17.

74. Ibid., p. 27.

75. Charles L. Heatherly, ed., *Mandate for Leadership: Policy Management in a Conservative Administration* (Washington, D.C.: Heritage Foundation, 1981), p. 1047.

76. Eliot Carlson, "Labor and the Humanities," *Humanities Report* 3 (May 1981): 10.

77. Ibid., p. 14.

78. Ibid.

79. *Washington Post,* Sept. 3, 1980, p. B2.

80. Carlson, "Labor and the Humanities," p. 9.

81. See *Humanities* 1 (July/Aug. 1980): 11-12.

82. *Washington Post,* Sept. 15, 1980, "Washington Business" section, p. 1.

83. *1980 Report,* p. 124.

84. Ibid.

85. *Congressional Record,* Senate, 96th Cong., 1st sess. (Aug. 8, 1978), p. S12845.

86. *Humanities* 1 (May/June 1980): 20.

87. *NEH Program Announcement, 1981-82,* p. 27.

88. Richard A. Harrison, "Newspaper Courses," *Humanities Report* 2 (Apr. 1980): 7.

89. Hugh Kenner, "Classics by the Pound," *Harper's,* Aug. 1982, pp. 70-73.

90. Fussell cited in Barbara Delman Wolfson, "The Role of the Scholar in Public Programs," *Humanities* 1 (July/Aug. 1980): 17.

91. Robert Hollander, "State Committees Should Emphasize 'Real Humanities,'" *Humanities Report* 4 (Feb. 1982): 3.

CHAPTER 9

1. Joint Hearings, *Arts and Humanities Bills,* p. 373.

2. Gordon N. Ray, "The Climate of Support for the Humanities" (paper

delivered at a conference on "The Future of the Humanities," Bad Homburg, Germany, July 2, 1981), p. 1.

3. *1980 Report,* p. xi.

4. Ann Hulbert, "The Well-Endowed Arts," *New Republic,* Aug. 15, 1981, p. 14.

5. Joseph Duffey, "Remarks at the Annual Meeting of ACLS," *ACLS Newsletter* 32 (Winter-Spring 1981): 11.

6. *The Letters of Gustave Flaubert, 1830-1857,* ed. Francis Steegmuller (Cambridge, Mass.: Harvard Univ. Press, 1979), p. 206.

7. Ray, "Climate of Support," p. 17.

8. Lumiansky cited in Douglas Taylor, *The Role of the Humanities in a Democratic Society* (Indianapolis: Poynter Center of Indiana Univ., 1978), p. 10.

9. Meyers, *Mind of the Founder,* p. 438.

10. *Chronicle of Higher Education,* Oct. 11, 1976, p. 9.

11. *Wall Street Journal,* Mar. 27, 1981, p. 27.

12. Stanley F. Turesky, "The Evaluation and Studies Branch of NEH," *ACLS Newsletter* 32 (Winter-Spring 1981): 18.

13. U.S., Congress, House, *National Foundation on the Arts and Humanities,* 91st Cong., 2d sess. (Mar. 23, 1970), p. 39.

14. Hulbert, "Well-Endowed Arts," p. 14.

15. *New York Times,* July 28, 1981, p. C3.

16. *Newsweek,* Oct. 13, 1980, p. 114.

17. E.D. Hirsch, Jr., "The Contents of English Literature," *Times Literary Supplement,* Dec. 10, 1982, p. 1360.

18. Bernard Bailyn, "The Challenge of Modern Historiography," *American Historical Review* 87 (Feb. 1982): 3.

19. *New York Times,* Dec. 14, 1982, p. C4.

20. *Chronicle of Higher Education,* Nov. 25, 1981, p. 1.

21. *Washington Star,* Mar. 1, 1981, p. F2.

22. *Washington Post,* Feb. 26, 1981, p. B1.

23. *Humanities Report* 4 (June 1982): 7.

24. *Newsweek,* Dec. 27, 1982, p. 13.

25. *Humanities Report* 4 (June 1982): 7.

26. Ray, "Climate of Support," p. 12.

27. *1980 Report,* p. 157.

28. Geoffrey Marshall, "The Humanities and the Federal Government," *Humanities* 2 (Oct. 1981): 21.

29. Steven J. Womack and Kristen J. Amundson, "Foundation Support for the Humanities," *Humanities Report* 4 (June 1982): 5.

30. "The Impact of NEH Programs" (unpublished NEH report, June 16, 1980), p. 1.

31. Ibid., p. 5.

INDEX